BOLLINGEN SERIES LXXI

THE

COLLECTED DIALOGUES OF

PLATO

INCLUDING THE LETTERS

Edited by

EDITH HAMILTON

and

HUNTINGTON CAIRNS

With Introduction and Prefatory Notes

BOLLINGEN SERIES LXXI

PANTHEON BOOKS

Published by BOLLINGEN FOUNDATION, *New York, N. Y.*
Distributed by
PANTHEON BOOKS, *a Division of* RANDOM HOUSE, INC., *New York, N. Y.*

THIS IS THE SEVENTY-FIRST
IN A SERIES OF BOOKS
SPONSORED AND PUBLISHED BY
BOLLINGEN FOUNDATION
Second printing, with corrections, March 1963
Third printing, October 1964
Fourth printing, October 1966

Library of Congress Catalogue Card No. 61–11758
Manufactured in the United States of America
DESIGNED BY ANDOR BRAUN

Translators

Lane Cooper · F. M. Cornford · W. K. C. Guthrie

R. Hackforth · Michael Joyce · Benjamin Jowett

L. A. Post · W. H. D. Rouse · Paul Shorey

J. B. Skemp · A. E. Taylor · Hugh Tredennick

W. D. Woodhead · J. Wright

CONTENTS

EDITORIAL NOTE

The notes which preface each of the dialogues were written by Miss Edith Hamilton.

The translations comprising this edition have been subject to only slight editing. The following general revisions may be noted. All commentaries, summaries, and footnotes of the original texts have been omitted. (In Theaetetus *and* Sophist, *the translator's summaries have been replaced by the text of Jowett's translation, third edition.) Spelling and, to some degree, punctuation and capitalization have been standardized, in accordance with American preferences. For measurements, money, etc., the Greek terms have been substituted for modern equivalents (such as furlong and shilling). Occasionally, where clarity would be served, Greek words and phrases have been inserted in brackets. Quotation marks are not used to set off speeches, but the use or nonuse of speakers' names has been left as it was. In addition, footnotes have usually been added to identify quotations.*

The index is based on the Abbott-Knight index to the third edition of Jowett's translation, though it has been entirely remade to answer the requirements of the present edition. An attempt has been made, by means of cross-references, to assist the reader with the philosophical vocabulary of the different translators. The index is the work of Edward J. Foye. The chief work of preparing the contents of this volume for the press has been done by Mrs. Donna Bishop under the supervision of the editors of Bollingen Series. The editors also are indebted to Mrs. Mabel A. Barry for special editorial assistance and other help.

*

Acknowledgment is gratefully made to the following publishers and persons for the use of the contents of this volume:

R. Hackforth's translations of Philebus *(1945) and* Phaedrus *(1952), by permission of the Cambridge University Press, Cambridge and New York, publishers.*

Benjamin Jowett's translations of Charmides, Laches, Timaeus, *and* Greater Hippias, *in the fourth edition, revised by order of the Jowett Copyright Trustees (1953), by permission of the Clarendon Press, Oxford. Jowett's translations of* Menexenus, Lesser Hippias, *and* Cratylus, *and excerpts of his translations of* Theaetetus *and*

Sophist *are from the third edition* (1892), *also published by the Clarendon Press.*

Lane Cooper's *translations of* Ion *and* Euthyphro (*copyright respectively 1938 and 1941 by him*), *by permission of Professor Cooper and of the Cornell University Press, Ithaca, New York, publishers.*

A. E. Taylor's *translation of* Laws (1934), J. Wright's *translation of* Lysis (1910), *and Michael Joyce's translation of* Symposium (1935), *by permission of J. M. Dent and Sons, London, and E. P. Dutton and Co., New York, publishers of these works in Everyman's Library.*

Paul Shorey's *translation of* Republic (1930), *by permission of the Harvard University Press, Cambridge, Mass., publishers, and the Trustees of the Loeb Classical Library.*

A. E. Taylor's *translation of* Critias (1929), *by permission of Methuen and Co., London, publishers.*

W. D. Woodhead's *translation of* Gorgias (1953) *and A. E. Taylor's translation of* Epinomis, *edited by Raymond Klibansky* (1956), *by permission of Thomas Nelson and Sons, Edinburgh and New York, publishers.*

Hugh Tredennick's *translations of* Apology, Crito, *and* Phaedo (1954) *and W. K. C. Guthrie's translations of* Protagoras *and* Meno (1956), *by arrangement with Penguin Books, Harmondsworth, England, publishers.*

L. A. Post's *translation of the* Epistles (1925), *by permission of Professor Post.*

W. H. D. Rouse's *translation of* Euthydemus, *here first published, by permission of Mr. Philip G. Rouse and Mr. J. C. G. Rouse. Acknowledgment is gratefully made to the New American Library of World Literature, New York, for assistance in this connection.*

F. M. Cornford's *translations of* Theaetetus *and* Sophist (1935) *and* Parmenides (1939), *by permission of Routledge and Kegan Paul, London, publishers.*

J. B. Skemp's *translation of* Statesman (1952), *by permission of Professor Skemp, the Yale University Press, New Haven, and Routledge and Kegan Paul, London, publishers.*

INTRODUCTION

THESE DIALOGUES were written twenty-three hundred years ago, and the thought of the ancient world, the Middle Ages, the Renaissance, and that of contemporary times, have all come under their influence. They have been praised as the substance of Western thought, as the corrective for the excesses to which the human mind is subject, and as setting forth the chief lines of the Western view of the world as they have never been delineated before or since in philosophy, politics, logic, and psychology. It has been held that a return to the insights of the dialogues is a return to our roots. But the dialogues have also had their enemies. They have been attacked as politically aristocratic and as philosophically mystical. However, few serious and fair students of the dialogues have ever denied their suggestiveness and the extent to which they stimulate thought. Many strands are interwoven in the dialogues but always at the center as their meaning is the Greek insight that Reason, the *logos*, is nature steering all things from within. In this approach nature is neither supernatural nor material; it is an organic whole, and man is not outside nature but within it. By concentration on this point of view and its implications Greek thought and art achieved a clarity never equaled elsewhere and Plato became its supreme spokesman.

Plato has been presented to us as a man of the study, a weaver of idealistic dreams; he has also been held up as a man with great experience of the world. There is no denying that he was learned, fully aware of the intellectual currents of his day. The variety of the quotations and allusions which appear in the dialogues show that he had read the extant literature. His life covered the period from the Peloponnesian War and the death of Pericles to Philip's capture of Olynthus. He was born about 428 B.C. and died at the age of eighty or eighty-one about 348 B.C. His family was an ancient one with political connections in high places and it is reasonable to assume that he saw military service in his youth. He had a wide acquaintance with the prominent men of his time, traveled extensively abroad, and at the age of forty founded the Academy and directed its affairs until his death. Thereafter the Academy had a continuous life of nine hundred years, a longer life span than that of any other educational institution in the West. This is scarcely the portrait of an armchair philosopher spinning theories in a study lined with books from floor to ceiling. It still leaves open, however, the question of the extent of

Plato's actual grasp of worldly affairs. Not infrequently scholars with experiences in life comparable to those of Plato confess themselves helpless in the planning of concrete undertakings, although plainly Plato himself would not have made that admission. Plato's abilities must here be judged by the merits of the specific proposals he outlines in the dialogues. It is not necessary to read them closely to be impressed with his intense interest in the correction of social and political abuses. That many of his suggestions had intrinsic value is adequately attested by their subsequent adoption in educational and political practice and the persistence of their influence even to the present.

Plato nowhere offers an explanation of why he cast his writings in the dialogue form rather than in that of the reasoned treatise. In the *Phaedrus* he argues that writing is like painting; it has the appearance of life but if you ask it a question it preserves a solemn silence. The written word cannot explain itself if it is misunderstood. Writing, he concludes, is a pastime, a game, but a noble one in which a man may discourse seriously and merrily about justice and the like. He wrote mimes in his youth, and with the example before him of the Socratic method of leading men to knowledge by question and answer it was perhaps natural that he should adopt the form he did. At any rate it gave his poetic powers great latitude. He was a stylist of the first order and as a poet he was able to present philosophy dramatically. He believed as a philosopher that the world is pervaded by Reason, and that its beauty is an outward manifestation of its ultimate nature. The dialogue form permitted him to lead men to this insight, it permitted the playfulness and the bitterness, the irony and the fairness, for which the dialogues are also famous. It allowed him almost the freedom of the contemporary novelist. As a form it imposed no limitations on his poetic imagery, and it allowed him also the utmost philosophical seriousness. But notwithstanding his unrivaled mastery of the dialogue he never subordinated meaning to form. Contentless art, he held, is not art.

All this is not separate from but intertwined with his task as a philosopher. In the physical sciences hypotheses are tested by experimental means, but the philosopher's resource is thought in the form of a conversation with himself or others. The dialogue form therefore is not arbitrarily chosen, not a report of how Greeks conversed on street corners, in the bath and the gymnasium, and certainly not an inquiry of the kind conducted in the assembly where many minds are assumed, somehow, to be the source of wisdom. On the contrary Plato held that inquiry, when not directed by one who knows, is futile. The dialogue therefore is the dialectic, a skillfully directed technique of questioning. For this reason he described the dialectician as the midwife tending us in the act, in the "labor," of knowing. To change the metaphor, the dialectician is like the gardener who aids his plants but is unable to do for them what they must do themselves.

This is the content, and the instrument which leads us to knowledge is the form. For Plato it is the one certain way to knowledge. Its effectiveness lies in the effort it demands on the part of the participants, and its achievement, as in the case of the plant, is fulfillment. In fact, the essence of Platonism may be said to be the realization that we can and must know, not by trial and error, which teaches too late, if indeed it teaches much at all, but by coming to see what is possible, and what is not possible, in the world in which we live. In Aristotle's view Plato's form was halfway between poetry and prose.

Plato was a philosopher and poet, but not a mystic. He was a poet in the sense that he wrote formal verse and is the author of one of the most notable of the Greek epigrams. Beyond that, as the author of the dialogues, he was a philosopher-poet exercising consummate artistry in his presentation of ideas. In this respect he differs from Lucretius, Dante, Pope, and others who have attempted to set forth in verse systems of thought not their own. If we put aside the requirement that poetry must be written in meter Plato is one of the supreme poets of the world as well as of Greece; he has a place with Homer, Aeschylus, and Dante, although no one of these men is also a philosopher. But his poetic insight has often been confused with mysticism, even with mysticism's most obscurantist manifestations. His discussion of the one and the many, the doctrine of love and eternal beauty, the Demiurgos, and similar matters, have all been mistakenly used, by mystics and occultists, as grounds for their own doctrines. He has been a source of inspiration to many types of mysticism but his writings have been repeatedly misread. This misunderstanding has been greatly promoted and popularized by the writings of Philo and Plotinus. Philo claimed that Plato's Ideas and the Biblical angels are one and the same, and Plotinus' mysticism is actually called Neoplatonism. But Plato saw the world to be intelligible, that is, he held that system pervades all things. In order to indicate the nature of that reality he resorted to story, metaphor, and playfulness which have given comfort from time to time to esoteric writers. But the difference between Plato and the mysticism that has attached itself to his philosophy is essential. Plato's aim is to take the reader by steps, with as severe a logic as the conversational method permits, to an insight into the ultimate necessity of Reason. And he never hesitates to submit his own ideas to the harshest critical scrutiny; he carried this procedure so far in the *Parmenides* that some commentators have held that his own doubts in this dialogue prevail over his affirmations. But the beliefs of mystics are not products of critical examination and logical clarification; they are, on the contrary, a series of apprehensions, flashes, based on feeling, denying the rational order. The mystic's reports of his experiences are beyond discussion inasmuch as they are subjective and emotional; they must be accepted, by one who wishes to believe them, as a matter of faith, not knowledge. Plato's view of the world is that of an intelligible system that man can know by disciplined intellect alone. He was, in fact, the founder of logic, a logician and a poet, but he was not a mystic, he never exalted feeling above reason.

In several senses Plato was an aristocrat, but not in the opprobrious sense of some of his critics. His family on both his father's and his mother's side was a distinguished one and had produced men sufficiently able to assume the obligations of leadership. Plato accepted the responsibility of his inherited position. His dominant aim was to prevent the further disintegration of Greece. Two courses were open to him, either the assumption of public office or the re-establishment of the clarity of the Greek intellect which had become corrupted by many influences. The fate of Socrates perhaps suggested to him that his special strength lay in the restoration of the Greek view of life. His position in the *Republic* is that good government can be conserved only by statesmen with knowledge in proportion to their task. In the *Laws* he attempted a more direct approach through the formulation of a specific legislative program. He was also aristocratic in the lifelong discipline with which he held himself to this task. His view that the final stage of the statesman's education should not be undertaken before the age of fifty would have little support today in conjunction with our desperate efforts at mass education. In Plato's hands aristocracy meant the rule of the best, from whatever class they came. The able were to receive special training for the responsibilities requiring great ability; the less able were to perform the tasks suitable to their ability. Plato's political theory is an implication of the system of nature, and to call this philosophy aristocratic is meaningful only in the sense that nature is itself aristocratic. But to call any philosophy aristocratic in the sense of class interest is meaningless; preoccupation with the interests of one class to the detriment of others is not philosophy. Philosophy is disinterested or it is not philosophy. When ideas are manipulated for personal ends, for class or group interests, the name for this in Plato's day was sophistry. It was against this that his dialogues were directed. To accuse Plato of being in league with the sophistic forces that undermined the classical world is an instance of the more subtle misrepresentation of his position. Plato's disinterested pursuit of knowledge has not only made the word *Platonism* synonymous with the word *philosophy*, it has marked him as the aristocrat of aristocrats, the paragon of excellence emulated by high-minded men for over two thousand years.

In the dialogues Plato appears to address himself to particular topics and in no one place in the conventional sense does he set forth a complete system of philosophy. This circumstance has prompted the view, especially during the nineteenth century, that the dialogues display an evolutionary development, that Plato gradually felt or thought his way to a final position which is displayed in the later writings. It has also led to the belief that as a philosopher he must have put forth a formal system and that it is now lost to us. We know that he lectured at the Academy and we have the authority of Aristotle that these lectures constituted "the philosophy of Plato." It is therefore argued that Platonism as a formal system was expounded in the lecture room very much in the manner of Aristotle. It may be so, but the notion is conjectural. The evolutionary view of the dialogues is also difficult to maintain. In them the same thoughts appear again and again, expressed in different words, in different contexts, and with varying emphasis. Plato was the culmination of several centuries of Greek speculation and he took full advantage of the insight which his predecessors had developed. But speculation assumes intelligibility. The insight that the world is system, is organic, therefore both orderly and alive, is the Greek view as far back as we have records. Because of this previous work in philosophy he was able relatively early in life to see the world as an entirety and to grapple with its implications. The Greek organic view stressed a living entirety made up of members. Plato's dialogues dealt with increasingly difficult problems but there is no shift in his convictions. His method throughout is one of exploration, of clarification, but the same insight dominates and the same principles recur. The world view they display is clear when the dialogues are seen as a whole. It is not stated all at once, or in any one place; it is unfolded gradually and its implications are explored. The important point is that the dialogues as a whole are alone a statement of his position. Plato was fully aware of the value of system in the search for knowledge, of the desirability of stating as clearly as possible the principles on which the inquiry turns. He chose a method quite distinct both from that of the positivist science of the present day which purports to start with the "facts," and from that of the deductive method of the system builders of the seventeenth century. But his approach on that account is no less rigorous and valid. His system unfolds as a flower unfolds, and halfway in its development we see its center, the *Republic,* holding the many petals firmly. Later, when the system has fully flowered, its periphery may well be said to be the *Laws.* He does not treat the various topics of his discourse, such as ethics, psychology, epistemology, as meaningful in themselves, but as organic, interrelated subjects meaningful only as variations upon a single theme. In this respect he differs from scientists who see the different departments of inquiry as having their own special components.

At the heart of Plato's philosophy is the doctrine of Ideas. It is the great discovery in the history of philosophy, and although it is the subject of extensive discussion in accounts of Plato's thought, the actual amount of space devoted to it by this name in the dialogues is scanty. Nevertheless it is the basic assumption behind everything he wrote. Thus Plato's technique combined example with exposition; to grasp fully what he intended to say about the theory of Ideas the dialogues must be understood as acts of knowing, examples of how knowledge is acquired. Expositions of Plato's position in treatise form can therefore be misleading. According to Aristotle, Plato accepted Heraclitus' doctrine that things, as we are aware of them through our organs of touch, taste, sight, and hearing, are all in constant flux and therefore our sense organs cannot give us knowledge. If the dominant color of a painting is one thing under the northern light of the sky and a different thing under artificial illumination it is apparent that the information we derive from our senses varies with conditions. Aristotle says that Plato was thus led to the view that if we are to have knowledge it must be of permanent entities distinct from those we know through the senses. Plato generally called these entities *Forms* or *Ideas,* terms which are misleading in English but which are now standard usage in Platonic studies. Today the word "idea" carries a subjective connotation, and the word "form" may be taken to mean form itself whereas Plato was talking about the principle of form. There has been a vast discussion of the nature of these entities, and Plato himself, as one dialogue followed another, touched on the question from many points of view. At one time they have been regarded by his critics as reified concepts and at another as ideas in the mind of God. Actually, however, they appear to be the ordering principle of which the world is constituted, the order in nature that all investigation seeks whether in physical science or in speculative philosophy. They are the meaning of the world of flux. The main point of Plato's argument is that the realm of Ideas is the reality of the objects which are ordered. What our senses report about objects is not wholly responsible and must be corrected by intelligence. All the sciences attempt to discover the laws which are the order of the phenomena in their particular fields. In physics, for example, the order is expressed by the laws of the conservation of energy, mass, momentum, gravitation, electric charge, and others, and in physiology by the laws of the general metabolism of the organism. In Platonism order is not the sum of the laws that science discovers but the principle of all laws, the *logos* or Intelligence itself. Plato approached this problem on the assumption that when we classify things under a general name we do so because permanence and order are there. Thus in the *Euthyphro, Charmides, Laches,* and the *Greater Hippias* the inquiry concerns the class, the Idea. The questions asked are, What is piety? What is temperance? What is courage? What is beauty? In the *Euthyphro* Socrates observes that there are many instances of piety but that he is searching for the Idea, the permanent, that which makes pious acts pious. From this elementary beginning in an exploration of the meaning of class names Plato passed on in the later dialogues to more sophisticated statements of his doctrine and its applicability to all aspects of the world. He saw it as the refutation of the view that all is flux and that man is the measure of things. These latter notions have recurred calling themselves naturalism, pragmatism, positivism, analysis, and existentialism. Plato's theory of Ideas is difficult to grasp in its full implications and while it can be stated its meaning is not obvious and will be understood only upon reflection. He has no doubt that the Ideas exist outside the human mind, and shows that by turning our attention to ultimate problems we attain knowledge, for our intelligence, like the eye, beholds that toward which it is turned; if we do not look we do not see.

Plato's artistry and philosophical power are nowhere shown to better advantage than in his discussion of friendship and love. Here he was venturing into a domain which poets have thought to be their special province but he took the subject further than it had been taken by any predecessor. More, he placed it on a basis from which the poetry of the West has derived sustenance to the present. In the *Lysis* Socrates and his companions endeavor to determine whether friendship or love is the attraction of likes or opposites, a theme of the novelist from *Daphnis and Chloë* to Proust and Joyce. Plato leaves the question unresolved in the *Lysis* but argues that friendship must have a purpose, and he identifies this purpose with the highest purpose—individual wholeness—the good. In the *Phaedrus* he discusses the madness of the lover, his struggle with appetite, and his desire to mold his beloved into the image of the Idea. At the end of this dialogue, when the discussion is over, Socrates addresses Pan praying for the beauty toward which the discussion has led.

Beloved Pan, and all ye other gods who haunt this place, give me beauty in the inward soul; and may the outward and the inward man be at one. May I reckon the wise to be the wealthy, and may I have such a quantity of gold as a temperate man and he only can bear and carry.

In the *Symposium* Plato carries the phenomenon of love from physical desire through the artistic impulse manifested in the way we do things (this includes the organization of States), to the love of the beautiful or Good which is the Idea that molds the world. It is this aspect of Plato's thought which received great attention in the sixteenth and seventeenth centuries and which passed into romantic literature as the vulgar notion of "Platonic love." The utilitarianism of today is more occupied with the proposals in the *Republic* and the *Laws* for the regulation of marriage and the enforcement of monogamy, but in the classical tradition Plato's doctrine of Eros or Love is seen for what it is, namely, as an integral part of his philosophy binding all things, making each a distinct whole.

Plato's doctrine of the soul, which has been associated with the Pythagoreans and the Orphic Mysteries in one direction, and was extended by Neoplatonism and Christianity in another, remains one of the perplexing puzzles in his philosophy. In his cosmology he allots to the soul forms of existence, sameness, and difference intermediate between the real being of the Ideas and physical objects. Since the soul is akin to the Ideas it is immortal; it is the chief author of change in physical bodies. Plato thus clearly believed in the imperishability of the soul (*psyche*) as the activating principle of change. Physical objects come and go but the activating power of Being is constant. In one of the greatest of all the dialogues, the *Phaedo,* Plato discussed the question of the immortality of the human soul in the sense of the survival of human consciousness after death. There are also references and arguments with respect to the same issue in other dialogues. None of the arguments is conclusive as Plato himself must have been aware, and as numerous commentators since his day have pointed out. It cannot be shown that Plato believed in immortality in this sense, and the precise meaning of his doctrine of the soul has been endlessly debated from ancient times to the present both on the basis of the text and from the implications of his philosophy as a whole. The problem has never been resolved and it appears unlikely that it ever will be. At the heart, however, of the doctrine was the insistence upon the supreme duty of "tending the soul" and making it as perfect as possible. By this Plato meant that it is man's obligation to know, to grasp the meaning of the world rationally, and to manage his conduct in accordance with that insight. In the myths he assumes the immortality of the individual soul but this may be understood, not as the affirmation of a truth, but as a necessary regulative principle in the State. At the end of the *Laws* he touches on the problem for the final time. The great lesson about death, he says, is that the soul is superior to the body, and that it is the soul which makes us what we are. In death man departs to render his account to the gods. Not much help can be given him now. While he was alive he should have been aided to live the good life by all connected with him so that after death he would have nothing to fear.

But the problem of individual immortality is only one aspect of Plato's treatment of the soul. To begin with, the word "soul," with its accretions of meanings during the centuries, is an unfortunate translation of the Greek word *psyche*. It is more properly translated, according to the various contexts, as Reason, Mind, Intelligence, Life, the vital principle in things as well as in man; it is the constant that causes change but itself does not change. In fact, Plato's use of many different words for the rational order has caused much confusion. One explanation of his use of different words suggests that he hoped to make us realize that meaning lies not in words but only in that for which words stand. Another likely explanation is that no one word is adequate to account for the ideational nature of reality. In any event, the soul, because it is Intelligence, is tripartite; it is one and also many and the proportion that fuses them.

Plato therefore associated his theory of the State with the tripartite nature of the soul. He remarks that the State does not spring from oaks or rocks but from the characters of its citizens. Nevertheless the connections that exist between the elements that comprise human nature and those that make up the structure of the State are, he warns us, to be taken only analogically; it is not a proof but a method that will be helpful in disclosing the essential nature of the State. Plato's theory of human nature is a complicated one and his tripartite division of it into human intelligence, courage, and appetite is not an instance of a primitive psychology. The division was made for the purpose in hand and was not intended to be exhaustive. Plato works out in considerable detail the connections between the appetitive aspect of human nature, its desires and wants on the one side, and the economic class on the other. Similarly he associates the courageous element with the military class. This division of human nature is represented by the fighting instinct in man, his competitiveness, and his sense of injustice. Finally, the rational or philosophical element is connected with the governing class. In a famous image Plato compares man's intelligence to a charioteer driving two horses, one spirited and one sluggish, but the three forming a unit. The just man, Plato therefore says, is governed by intelligence even as the just State is governed by its most intelligent members.

Plato's theory of art, like everything he wrote, is an implication of the doctrine of Ideas. To him the world was a living system of Ideas and, true to this view, he never treats aspects of knowledge in isolation. We, as part of this system, know potentially; he therefore tries to lead us to see for ourselves. This has prompted some scholars to imagine that he leaves, not only philosophy itself but the theory of art, unanchored and unsystematic. But each dialogue, although exploring a different aspect of knowledge, has within it, by implication, the whole of knowledge as he envisaged it. In the *Timaeus*— Plato's poetic account of the universe—God is the Demiurgos, the craftsman, and the world is his product. He is the artist working toward fully understood ends, he is Intelligence forming all things from within. Thus when man understands the world he too can be an artist in all that he does. This is man's distinctive function, and the essential artist is the Statesman. Art is imitation, not of things, but of the nature of things, and man is an imitator, not a creator. Dante carried on this tradition when he wrote, "Art is the grandchild of God."

Much has been made of Plato's criticism of the poets, particularly of Homer, Hesiod, and the tragic drama. He criticized them for what he considered their excesses. Zeus should not have been pictured as subject to love potions administered by the scheming Hera, and Achilles' grief over the death of Patroclus Plato thought excessive; in tragic drama too he found excesses of emotion. Excess, he held, violates proportion and makes bad art and bad ethics. He concluded that the arts, so effective for good or evil, should be guided by the more intelligent members of the State, the philosophers, whose concern, training, and innate ability best equip them for that function. He was not hostile to art or poetry as such but only to unintelligent art, for he would not admit that imagination had a claim to the allegiance of men superior to the claim of intellect. "Let our artists," he wrote, "rather be those who are gifted to discern the true nature of the beautiful and graceful; then will our youth dwell in a land of health, amid fair sights and sounds, and receive the good in everything; and beauty, the effluence of fair works, shall flow into the eye and ear, like a health-giving breeze from a purer region, and insensibly draw the soul from earliest years into likeness and sympathy with the beauty of reason." No one has seen more deeply than Plato the beneficent effects of great art, but he argues that unfettered imagination and formless intuitionalism lead to error. Emotion like all things is beneficial when in balance, but art out of balance is not art. The great poet is one who does not misrepresent the world, but who discloses its real nature.

When Plato turned his attention to moral and political problems he did so from the point of view of his theory of Ideas. His purpose is to show that ethics and politics can be studied rationally if approached from the vantage ground which his philosophy gives us. In his view ethics and politics are indivisible implications of the natural order. He was not interested in describing existing states inasmuch as he thought they were all bad. He wanted to discover the real nature of the State, what it necessarily is if its full purpose is realized. This has always been the practice of even the most advanced sciences which proceed on the basis of ideal entities such as frictionless engines, perfect levers, perfectly rigid bodies, and similar constructions. Plato believed that a state, like all other things, possesses certain characteristics or it does not function properly and it was his intention to examine them. His standard, the rational order, conditions the structure and practices of the State. Evidence for this lies in the need men have for the different abilities of different individuals. The State is therefore a system of reciprocal services. This implies Plato's second great principle, the division of labor or specialization of function. Each man will perform the task for which he is best suited and the surplus of his product will be exchanged for the surplus of other specialists. In this way political life conserves its natural unity. Too often, political groups lose their unity by becoming divided into camps, rich and poor; but if each man cultivates his own abilities, such as they are, he will be happy and healthy, and the State will be healthy and whole. It is important to recognize that the political standard is the opposite of uniformity since different capacities are needed and each member has the greatest possible latitude to develop his own different abilities.

Owing to the necessity of difference Plato recognized three classes of men: the workers, merchants, traders, and businessmen who make up the bulk of the population, whose interest and therefore function is economic, supplying the material needs of the State; and the guardians, consisting of two classes, the statesmen who manage the public affairs and the soldiers and educators who protect the State against its internal and external enemies. The members of the three classes are born with differentiated interests which should be trained for their own individual fulfillment and happiness, and they will find their way to their proper occupation through their natural inclinations and abilities helped by educational facilities. Plato recognizes that this is a class, not a caste system, since the individual's position is not founded on heredity but on demonstrated qualities. At the peak of the system is the statesman, the man who has a grasp of the scheme of things. In the course of his argument Plato develops elaborate views on the conservation of this order by control of wealth, the regulation and equality of the sexes, education, and the place of art in political life. His analysis of the political order has found proponents and antagonists in succeeding ages, and it is clear that the problems he discussed are the problems that do not change. In the *Republic*, which he wrote in middle age, he found that with intelligent leadership and with the educational advantages of a healthy political life there would be little need for positive law. But in the *Laws* written at the end of his life, he is concerned with the alternative to intelligent leadership—the need for a few necessary laws clearly stated and firmly enforced.

His argument reaches one of its peaks in his defense of the natural order as justice. He means no more than what he has already said. Justice is realized in political life when the members of the State discharge their proper functions excellently and do not assume tasks beyond their competence. Justice is the principle which makes the State a whole and maintains its parts in due proportion. Through the observance of this principle both the State and the individual can achieve a satisfactory life. This alone gives the State its meaning, its proportion, what, in its absence, would cause it to perish. The principle of justice is the principle of the State, for the State has no other end than the conservation of its natural order.

It is evident that Plato's explorations were conducted on the basis of a firm grasp of logical principles. Unlike Aristotle he did not put forward a systematic account of logical rules, and in that sense he did not see logic as a discipline possessing a distinct subject matter. But the revival of interest in logical studies, which has been a feature of contemporary thought, has brought about a corresponding concern with its development in the hands of ancient Greek thinkers. There have been efforts to show that on important points, such as the logic of the syllogism, the concept, and judgments, Plato was the first to work out the general theory. When he touches on logical matters Plato's vocabulary, as in his mathematical discussions, can on occasion be technical in the extreme. It is the writing of a man who is a master of his subject matter.

It is also evident that Plato saw logic as more than an instrument. It was the essence of philosophy because it sought to discover the invariant laws of being, those necessities grounded in nature against which, as he says, not even the gods contend. Those logical truths, such as the relation of incompatibility or the principle of identity, are expressions of something that obtains in the external world; they are more objectively true than the circumstance that physical science affirms. They are the invariants that constitute the order of the world. They are not comparable, as is sometimes alleged, to the rules of chess where we do not ask if a particular game is "true," but rather "was the game played in accordance with the rules?" In Plato's logic we do ask if it is true that a relation of incompatibility exists. We put that question because the absence of incompatibility in nature is evidence of its intelligibility. For this reason Plato's logic implies that logical truth is itself a principle of the order of nature.

After the "logical" dialogues Plato gave an account in the *Timaeus* of his views on cosmology. It is a myth and, as Plato says, no more than a "likely story." It is presented as a continuation of the *Republic,* and in ancient times, and even today, it is held to embody Plato's last thoughts on the ultimate nature of things. In part it is a reflection of the science and mathematics of his time, but it too is dominated by the idea that the universe is the product of Reason seeking to realize itself. In a key sentence Plato says that the world is a composite result generated by Reason and Necessity. Reason overruled Necessity by persuading her to conduct to the best end the greater part of things. By this he seems to mean that the intelligibility of the world is due to the imposition on certain necessities of nature, its "errant causes," of a directing or teleological principle. This distinction between Reason and Necessity is one of the peculiarities of the *Timaeus* which perhaps caused Hegel to deny that it could have been written by Plato; it was, he argued, an old Pythagorean manuscript. Plato's own philosophy rests on the doctrine that at the heart of things there is Intelligence at work endeavoring everywhere to fulfill itself. The *Timaeus* must be read as a poem, more profound in its insight than the *De rerum natura* of Lucretius since it allowed for all that Lucretius described and made it plain that the materialist view is insufficient to account for the world.

Although the *Timaeus* takes the form of a myth, a vision of the physical world, it should not be supposed that it is less profound than the other dialogues. In the *Timaeus* Plato's aim is to reveal order in terms of the world of things. But notwithstanding its mythical form, or perhaps because of it, the *Timaeus* has been one of Plato's most influential dialogues. However, it is a dangerous undertaking to make the *Timaeus* or other writings of Plato say more than Plato intended or to interpret his remarks as anticipations of later developments. The Christian Fathers and the Middle Ages found in the first sentence of the *Timaeus* a foreknowledge of the Trinity. We are told in our own sophisticated age by a responsible historian of science that Plato himself formulated the idea of negative numbers and that he advanced the germ of the Newtonian-Leibnizian calculus. We are also told that the theory of Ideas is a counterpart of contemporary mathematical logic. Today the Copenhagen quantum physicists argue that the views of Plato in the *Timaeus* more closely approximate the fundamental law of nature than those of his opponents in the classical world. The *Timaeus* is a poem on the inauguration of the world, penetrating, compact, and great in conception. Whatever anticipations of contemporary knowledge it may disclose neither add to nor subtract from its importance as Plato's effort at a comprehensive vision of nature. His own insight is elaborated in other dialogues and it is by the truth or falsity of that insight that he must stand or fall.

Plato's philosophy is unique in the history of thought since what he said has been stated only once. His great commentators from Aristotle to Hegel have all attempted to improve upon him. He was poet, thinker, scientist all in one and there has been no such combination of powers displayed by anyone before or since. To understand Plato is to be educated; it is to see the nature of the world in which we live. The vitality of what he has to say is due to one factor. He took his point of departure from what is and not from what man wants. One by one he took up the great problems and if he did not solve them he left them at least in a framework in which subsequent ages could see them in their essential nature. He has been misunderstood, and adapted to points of view completely antithetical to his own; but these aberrations have always run their course, and it is by a return to Plato's insights that the thought of the West has continually renewed itself.

H. C.

THE COLLECTED DIALOGUES
OF PLATO

SOCRATES' DEFENSE

(APOLOGY)

The first three dialogues given here are an account of the last days and the death of Socrates. In what order Plato wrote the dialogues we do not know, but in reading them there is a good reason for beginning with those that center in the death of the chief personage. Only in them is Socrates himself the subject. In the others, although almost always the main speaker, he rarely speaks of himself. Indeed, in two of the three latest dialogues he is only a listener, and in the last he does not even appear. But in these first three he talks at length about his life and his beliefs.

In his Defense, Socrates explains himself to his fellow citizens when he is brought before an Athenian court on a most serious charge. "Socrates is guilty of corrupting the minds of the young, and of believing in deities of his own invention instead of the gods recognized by the state." In the Apology, as it is generally known, he gives a detailed account of the way he has lived and the convictions he has reached.

At the end, when he is condemned to death, the few words in which he accepts the sentence are in themselves a vivid picture of the man he was, unlike any other there has ever been. Great spiritual leaders and great saints adorn the pages of history, but Socrates is not like any of them. He is, indeed, the servant of the divine power, living in complete obedience to God; yet he always views the world of men with a bit of humor, a touch of irony. He spends his life in the effort to kindle into a flame the spark of good in every man, but when he fails, when he comes up against blind obstinacy or stupid conceit or the indifference of egotism, or when he draws down on himself bitter enmity, then along with his regret—because he cares for everyone— is mingled a little amusement, a feeling, as it were, of rueful sympathy, as if he said to himself, "What silly children we are." Socrates never condemned.

This significant clue to what he was is given most clearly in Socrates' Defense.

3

17 I do not know what effect my accusers have had upon you, gentlemen, but for my own part I was almost carried away by them—their arguments were so convincing. On the other hand, scarcely a word of what they said was true. I was especially astonished at one of their many misrepresentations; I mean when they told you that you must be careful not to let me deceive you—the implication being that I am

b a skillful speaker. I thought that it was peculiarly brazen of them to tell you this without a blush, since they must know that they will soon be effectively confuted, when it becomes obvious that I have not the slightest skill as a speaker—unless, of course, by a skillful speaker they mean one who speaks the truth. If that is what they mean, I would agree that I am an orator, though not after their pattern.

My accusers, then, as I maintain, have said little or nothing that is true, but from me you shall hear the whole truth—not, I can assure you, gentlemen, in flowery language like theirs, decked out with fine

c words and phrases. No, what you will hear will be a straightforward speech in the first words that occur to me, confident as I am in the justice of my cause, and I do not want any of you to expect anything different. It would hardly be suitable, gentlemen, for a man of my age to address you in the artificial language of a schoolboy orator. One thing, however, I do most earnestly beg and entreat of you. If you hear me defending myself in the same language which it has been my habit to use, both in the open spaces of this city—where many of you have heard me—and elsewhere, do not be surprised, and do not inter-

d rupt. Let me remind you of my position. This is my first appearance in a court of law, at the age of seventy, and so I am a complete stranger to the language of this place. Now if I were really from another country, you would naturally excuse me if I spoke in the manner and

18 dialect in which I had been brought up, and so in the present case I make this request of you, which I think is only reasonable, to disregard the manner of my speech—it may be better or it may be worse —and to consider and concentrate your attention upon this one question, whether my claims are fair or not. That is the first duty of the juryman, just as it is the pleader's duty to speak the truth.

The proper course for me, gentlemen of the jury, is to deal first with the earliest charges that have been falsely brought against me, and with my earliest accusers, and then with the later ones. I make

b this distinction because I have already been accused in your hearing by a great many people for a great many years, though without a word of truth, and I am more afraid of those people than I am of Anytus and his colleagues, although they are formidable enough. But the others are still more formidable. I mean the people who took hold of so many of you when you were children and tried to fill your minds with

From *The Last Days of Socrates*, translated and with an introduction by Hugh Tredennick (Penguin Classics, Harmondsworth, Middlesex, 1954).

untrue accusations against me, saying, There is a wise man called
Socrates who has theories about the heavens and has investigated
everything below the earth, and can make the weaker argument defeat
the stronger.

It is these people, gentlemen, the disseminators of these rumors, c
who are my dangerous accusers, because those who hear them suppose that anyone who inquires into such matters must be an atheist.
Besides, there are a great many of these accusers, and they have been
accusing me now for a great many years. And what is more, they approached you at the most impressionable age, when some of you were
children or adolescents, and they literally won their case by default,
because there was no one to defend me. And the most fantastic
thing of all is that it is impossible for me even to know and tell you
their names, unless one of them happens to be a playwright. All these d
people, who have tried to set you against me out of envy and love of
slander—and some too merely passing on what they have been told by
others—all these are very difficult to deal with. It is impossible to
bring them here for cross-examination; one simply has to conduct
one's defense and argue one's case against an invisible opponent, because there is no one to answer. So I ask you to accept my statement
that my critics fall into two classes, on the one hand my immediate
accusers, and on the other those earlier ones whom I have mentioned, e
and you must suppose that I have first to defend myself against the
latter. After all, you heard them abusing me longer ago and much
more violently than these more recent accusers.

Very well, then, I must begin my defense, gentlemen, and I must
try, in the short time that I have, to rid your minds of a false impres- 19
sion which is the work of many years. I should like this to be the result, gentlemen, assuming it to be for your advantage and my own;
and I should like to be successful in my defense, but I think that it
will be difficult, and I am quite aware of the nature of my task. However, let that turn out as God wills. I must obey the law and make my
defense.

Let us go back to the beginning and consider what the charge is
that has made me so unpopular, and has encouraged Meletus to draw b
up this indictment. Very well, what did my critics say in attacking
my character? I must read out their affidavit, so to speak, as though
they were my legal accusers: Socrates is guilty of criminal meddling,
in that he inquires into things below the earth and in the sky, and
makes the weaker argument defeat the stronger, and teaches others
to follow his example. It runs something like that. You have seen it c
for yourselves in the play by Aristophanes, where Socrates goes whirl-
ing round, proclaiming that he is walking on air, and uttering a great
deal of other nonsense about things of which I know nothing whatso-
ever. I mean no disrespect for such knowledge, if anyone really is
versed in it—I do not want any more lawsuits brought against me by

Meletus—but the fact is, gentlemen, that I take no interest in it.
d What is more, I call upon the greater part of you as witnesses to my
statement, and I appeal to all of you who have ever listened to me
talking—and there are a great many to whom this applies—to clear
your neighbors' minds on this point. Tell one another whether any
one of you has ever heard me discuss such questions briefly or at
length, and then you will realize that the other popular reports about
me are equally unreliable.

The fact is that there is nothing in any of these charges, and if
you have heard anyone say that I try to educate people and charge a
e fee, there is no truth in that either. I wish that there were, because I
think that it is a fine thing if a man is qualified to teach, as in the
case of Gorgias of Leontini and Prodicus of Ceos and Hippias of
Elis. Each one of these is perfectly capable of going into any city and
actually persuading the young men to leave the company of their fel-
20 low citizens, with any of whom they can associate for nothing, and
attach themselves to him, and pay money for the privilege, and be
grateful into the bargain.

There is another expert too from Paros who I discovered was here
on a visit; I happened to meet a man who has paid more in Sophists'
fees than all the rest put together—I mean Callias, the son of Hip-
ponicus. So I asked him—he has two sons, you see—Callias, I said, if
your sons had been colts or calves, we should have had no difficulty
b in finding and engaging a trainer to perfect their natural qualities,
and this trainer would have been some sort of horse dealer or agri-
culturalist. But seeing that they are human beings, whom do you intend to get as their instructor? Who is the expert in perfecting the
human and social qualities? I assume from the fact of your having
sons that you must have considered the question. Is there such a person or not?

Certainly, said he.

Who is he, and where does he come from? said I. And what
does he charge?

Evenus of Paros, Socrates, said he, and his fee is five minas.
c I felt that Evenus was to be congratulated if he really was a master of this art and taught it at such a moderate fee. I should certainly
plume myself and give myself airs if I understood these things, but
in fact, gentlemen, I do not.

Here perhaps one of you might interrupt me and say, But
what is it that you do, Socrates? How is it that you have been mis-
represented like this? Surely all this talk and gossip about you would
never have arisen if you had confined yourself to ordinary activities,
but only if your behavior was abnormal. Tell us the explanation, if
d you do not want us to invent it for ourselves.

This seems to me to be a reasonable request, and I will try to explain to you what it is that has given me this false notoriety. So

please give me your attention. Perhaps some of you will think that I am not being serious, but I assure you that I am going to tell you the whole truth.

I have gained this reputation, gentlemen, from nothing more or less than a kind of wisdom. What kind of wisdom do I mean? Human wisdom, I suppose. It seems that I really am wise in this limited sense. Presumably the geniuses whom I mentioned just now are wise in a e wisdom that is more than human. I do not know how else to account for it. I certainly have no knowledge of such wisdom, and anyone who says that I have is a liar and willful slanderer. Now, gentlemen, please do not interrupt me if I seem to make an extravagant claim, for what I am going to tell you is not my own opinion. I am going to refer you to an unimpeachable authority. I shall call as witness to my wisdom, such as it is, the god at Delphi.

You know Chaerephon, of course. He was a friend of mine from 21 boyhood, and a good democrat who played his part with the rest of you in the recent expulsion and restoration. And you know what he was like, how enthusiastic he was over anything that he had once undertaken. Well, one day he actually went to Delphi and asked this question of the god—as I said before, gentlemen, please do not interrupt—he asked whether there was anyone wiser than myself. The priestess replied that there was no one. As Chaerephon is dead, the evidence for my statement will be supplied by his brother, who is here in court.

Please consider my object in telling you this. I want to explain to b you how the attack upon my reputation first started. When I heard about the oracle's answer, I said to myself, What does the god mean? Why does he not use plain language? I am only too conscious that I have no claim to wisdom, great or small. So what can he mean by asserting that I am the wisest man in the world? He cannot be telling a lie; that would not be right for him.

After puzzling about it for some time, I set myself at last with considerable reluctance to check the truth of it in the following way. I went to interview a man with a high reputation for wisdom, because I felt that here if anywhere I should succeed in disproving the c oracle and pointing out to my divine authority, You said that I was the wisest of men, but here is a man who is wiser than I am.

Well, I gave a thorough examination to this person—I need not mention his name, but it was one of our politicians that I was studying when I had this experience—and in conversation with him I formed the impression that although in many people's opinion, and especially in his own, he appeared to be wise, in fact he was not. Then when I began to try to show him that he only thought he was wise and was not really so, my efforts were resented both by him and by d many of the other people present. However, I reflected as I walked away, Well, I am certainly wiser than this man. It is only too likely that neither of us has any knowledge to boast of, but he thinks that he knows something which he does not know, whereas I am quite conscious of my ignorance. At any rate it seems that I am wiser than he is to this small extent, that I do not think that I know what I do not know.

e   After this I went on to interview a man with an even greater reputation for wisdom, and I formed the same impression again, and here too I incurred the resentment of the man himself and a number of others.

From that time on I interviewed one person after another. I realized with distress and alarm that I was making myself unpopular, but I felt compelled to put my religious duty first. Since I was trying to find out the meaning of the oracle, I was bound to interview everyone who had a reputation for knowledge. And by dog, gentlemen, for I

22 must be frank with you, my honest impression was this. It seemed to me, as I pursued my investigation at the god's command, that the people with the greatest reputations were almost entirely deficient, while others who were supposed to be their inferiors were much better qualified in practical intelligence.

I want you to think of my adventures as a sort of pilgrimage undertaken to establish the truth of the oracle once for all. After I had finished with the politicians I turned to the poets, dramatic, lyric, and

b   all the rest, in the belief that here I should expose myself as a comparative ignoramus. I used to pick up what I thought were some of their most perfect works and question them closely about the meaning of what they had written, in the hope of incidentally enlarging my own knowledge. Well, gentlemen, I hesitate to tell you the truth, but it must be told. It is hardly an exaggeration to say that any of the bystanders could have explained those poems better than their actual authors. So I soon made up my mind about the poets too. I decided

c   that it was not wisdom that enabled them to write their poetry, but a kind of instinct or inspiration, such as you find in seers and prophets who deliver all their sublime messages without knowing in the least what they mean. It seemed clear to me that the poets were in much the same case, and I also observed that the very fact that they were poets made them think that they had a perfect understanding of all other subjects, of which they were totally ignorant. So I left that line of inquiry too with the same sense of advantage that I had felt in the case of the politicians.

Last of all I turned to the skilled craftsmen. I knew quite well

d   that I had practically no technical qualifications myself, and I was sure that I should find them full of impressive knowledge. In this I was not disappointed. They understood things which I did not, and to that extent they were wiser than I was. But, gentlemen, these professional experts seemed to share the same failing which I had noticed in the poets. I mean that on the strength of their technical proficiency they claimed a perfect understanding of every other subject, however important, and I felt that this error more than outweighed their positive wisdom. So I made myself spokesman for the oracle, and asked myself whether I would rather be as I was—neither wise with e their wisdom nor stupid with their stupidity—or possess both qualities as they did. I replied through myself to the oracle that it was best for me to be as I was.

The effect of these investigations of mine, gentlemen, has been to arouse against me a great deal of hostility, and hostility of a 23 particularly bitter and persistent kind, which has resulted in various malicious suggestions, including the description of me as a professor of wisdom. This is due to the fact that whenever I succeed in disproving another person's claim to wisdom in a given subject, the bystanders assume that I know everything about that subject myself. But the truth of the matter, gentlemen, is pretty certainly this, that real wisdom is the property of God, and this oracle is his way of telling us that human wisdom has little or no value. It seems to me that he is not referring literally to Socrates, but has merely taken my name as b an example, as if he would say to us, The wisest of you men is he who has realized, like Socrates, that in respect of wisdom he is really worthless.

That is why I still go about seeking and searching in obedience to the divine command, if I think that anyone is wise, whether citizen or stranger, and when I think that any person is not wise, I try to help the cause of God by proving that he is not. This occupation has kept me too busy to do much either in politics or in my own affairs. In fact, my service to God has reduced me to extreme poverty.   c

There is another reason for my being unpopular. A number of young men with wealthy fathers and plenty of leisure have deliberately attached themselves to me because they enjoy hearing other people cross-questioned. These often take me as their model, and go on to try to question other persons. Whereupon, I suppose, they find an unlimited number of people who think that they know something, but really know little or nothing. Consequently their victims become annoyed, not with themselves but with me, and they complain that there is a pestilential busybody called Socrates who fills young people's heads with wrong ideas. If you ask them what he does, and what he d teaches that has this effect, they have no answer, not knowing what to say. But as they do not want to admit their confusion, they fall back on the stock charges against any philosopher, that he teaches his pupils about things in the heavens and below the earth, and to disbelieve in gods, and to make the weaker argument defeat the stronger. They would be very loath, I fancy, to admit the truth—which is that they are being convicted of pretending to knowledge when they are entirely ignorant. So, jealous, I suppose, for their own reputation, and e also energetic and numerically strong, and provided with a plausible and carefully worked-out case against me, these people have been dinning into your ears for a long time past their violent denunciations of myself.

There you have the causes which led to the attack upon me by Meletus and Anytus and Lycon, Meletus being aggrieved on behalf of the poets, Anytus on behalf of the professional men and politicians,
24 and Lycon on behalf of the orators. So, as I said at the beginning, I should be surprised if I were able, in the short time that I have, to rid your minds of a misconception so deeply implanted.

There, gentlemen, you have the true facts, which I present to you without any concealment or suppression, great or small. I am fairly certain that this plain speaking of mine is the cause of my unpopularity, and this really goes to prove that my statements are true, and that I have described correctly the nature and the grounds of the calumny which has been brought against me. Whether you in-
b quire into them now or later, you will find the facts as I have just described them.

So much for my defense against the charges brought by the first group of my accusers. I shall now try to defend myself against Meletus—high-principled and patriotic as he claims to be—and after that against the rest.

Let us first consider their deposition again, as though it represented a fresh prosecution. It runs something like this: Socrates is guilty of corrupting the minds of the young, and of believing in deities of his own invention instead of the gods recognized by the state.
c Such is the charge. Let us examine its points one by one.

First it says that I am guilty of corrupting the young. But I say, gentlemen, that Meletus is guilty of treating a serious matter with levity, since he summons people to stand their trial on frivolous grounds, and professes concern and keen anxiety in matters about which he has never had the slightest interest. I will try to prove this to your satisfaction.
d   Come now, Meletus, tell me this. You regard it as supremely important, do you not, that our young people should be exposed to the best possible influence?

I do.

Very well, then, tell these gentlemen who it is that influences the young for the better. Obviously you must know, if you are so much interested. You have discovered the vicious influence, as you say, in myself, and you are now prosecuting me before these gentlemen. Speak up and inform them who it is that has a good influence upon the young. . . . You see, Meletus, that you are tongue-tied and cannot answer. Do you not feel that this is discreditable, and a sufficient proof in itself of what I said, that you have no interest in the subject? Tell me, my friend, who is it that makes the young good?

The laws.

That is not what I mean, my dear sir. I am asking you to name e the *person* whose first business it is to know the laws.

These gentlemen here, Socrates, the members of the jury.

Do you mean, Meletus, that they have the ability to educate the young, and to make them better?

Certainly.

Does this apply to all jurymen, or only to some?

To all of them.

Excellent! A generous supply of benefactors. Well, then, do these spectators who are present in court have an improving influence, or not?

Yes, they do.   25

And what about the members of the Council?

Yes, the councilors too.

But surely, Meletus, the members of the Assembly do not corrupt the young? Or do all of them too exert an improving influence?

Yes, they do.

Then it would seem that the whole population of Athens has a refining effect upon the young, except myself, and I alone demoralize them. Is that your meaning?

Most emphatically, yes.

This is certainly a most unfortunate quality that you have detected in me. Well, let me put another question to you. Take the case of horses. Do you believe that those who improve them make up the whole of mankind, and that there is only one person who has a bad b effect on them? Or is the truth just the opposite, that the ability to improve them belongs to one person or to very few persons, who are horse trainers, whereas most people, if they have to do with horses and make use of them, do them harm? Is not this the case, Meletus, both with horses and with all other animals? Of course it is, whether you and Anytus deny it or not. It would be a singular dispensation of fortune for our young people if there is only one person who corrupts them, while all the rest have a beneficial effect. But I need say no more. There is ample proof, Meletus, that you have never bothered c your head about the young, and you make it perfectly clear that you have never taken the slightest interest in the cause for the sake of which you are now indicting me.

Here is another point. Tell me seriously, Meletus, is it better to live in a good or in a bad community? Answer my question, like a good fellow; there is nothing difficult about it. Is it not true that wicked people have a bad effect upon those with whom they are in the closest contact, and that good people have a good effect?

Quite true.

Is there anyone who prefers to be harmed rather than benefited d by his associates? Answer me, my good man; the law commands you to answer. Is there anyone who prefers to be harmed?

Of course not.

Well, then, when you summon me before this court for corrupting the young and making their characters worse, do you mean that I
do so intentionally or unintentionally?

I mean intentionally.

Why, Meletus, are you at your age so much wiser than I at
mine? You have discovered that bad people always have a bad effect,
e and good people a good effect, upon their nearest neighbors. Am I so
hopelessly ignorant as not even to realize that by spoiling the character of one of my companions I shall run the risk of getting some
harm from him? Because nothing else would make me commit this
grave offense intentionally. No, I do not believe it, Meletus, and I do
26 not suppose that anyone else does. Either I have not a bad influence,
or it is unintentional, so that in either case your accusation is false.
And if I unintentionally have a bad influence, the correct procedure in
cases of such involuntary misdemeanors is not to summon the cul-
prit before this court, but to take him aside privately for instruction
and reproof, because obviously if my eyes are opened, I shall stop doing
what I do not intend to do. But you deliberately avoided my company
in the past and refused to enlighten me, and now you bring me before
this court, which is the place appointed for those who need punishment, not for those who need enlightenment.

It is quite clear by now, gentlemen, that Meletus, as I said before,
b has never shown any degree of interest in this subject. However, I invite you to tell us, Meletus, in what sense you make out that I corrupt
the minds of the young. Surely the terms of your indictment make it
clear that you accuse me of teaching them to believe in new deities
instead of the gods recognized by the state. Is not that the teaching of
mine which you say has this demoralizing effect?

That is precisely what I maintain.

c Then I appeal to you, Meletus, in the name of these same gods
about whom we are speaking, to explain yourself a little more clearly
to myself and to the jury, because I cannot make out what your point
is. Is it that I teach people to believe in some gods—which implies
that I myself believe in gods, and am not a complete atheist, so that I
am not guilty on that score—but in different gods from those recognized by the state, so that your accusation rests upon the fact that
they are different? Or do you assert that I believe in no gods at all,
and teach others to do the same?

Yes, I say that you disbelieve in gods altogether.

You surprise me, Meletus. What is your object in saying that? Do
d you suggest that I do not believe that the sun and moon are gods, as
is the general belief of all mankind?

He certainly does not, gentlemen of the jury, since he says that
the sun is a stone and the moon a mass of earth.

Do you imagine that you are prosecuting Anaxagoras, my dear

Meletus? Have you so poor an opinion of these gentlemen, and do you assume them to be so illiterate as not to know that the writings of Anaxagoras of Clazomenae are full of theories like these? And do you seriously suggest that it is from me that the young get these ideas, when they can buy them on occasion in the market place for a drachma at most, and so have the laugh on Socrates if he claims e them for his own, to say nothing of their being so silly? Tell me honestly, Meletus, is that your opinion of me? Do I believe in no god?

No, none at all, not in the slightest degree.

You are not at all convincing, Meletus—not even to yourself, I suspect. In my opinion, gentlemen, this man is a thoroughly selfish bully, and has brought this action against me out of sheer wanton aggressiveness and self-assertion. He seems to be devising a sort of in- 27 telligence test for me, saying to himself, Will the infallible Socrates realize that I am contradicting myself for my own amusement, or shall I succeed in deceiving him and the rest of my audience?

It certainly seems to me that he is contradicting himself in this indictment, which might just as well run: Socrates is guilty of not believing in the gods, but believing in the gods. And this is pure flippancy.

I ask you to examine with me, gentlemen, the line of reasoning which leads me to this conclusion. You, Meletus, will oblige us by answering my questions. Will you all kindly remember, as I requested b at the beginning, not to interrupt if I conduct the discussion in my customary way?

Is there anyone in the world, Meletus, who believes in human activities, and not in human beings? Make him answer, gentlemen, and don't let him keep on making these continual objections. Is there anyone who does not believe in horses, but believes in horses' activities? Or who does not believe in musicians, but believes in musical activities? No, there is not, my worthy friend. If you do not want to answer, I will supply it for you and for these gentlemen too. But the next question you must answer. Is there anyone who believes in c supernatural activities and not in supernatural beings?

No.

How good of you to give a bare answer under compulsion by the court! Well, do you assert that I believe and teach others to believe in supernatural activities? It does not matter whether they are new or old. The fact remains that I believe in them according to your statement; indeed you solemnly swore as much in your affidavit. But if I believe in supernatural activities, it follows inevitably that I also believe in supernatural beings. Is not that so? It is. I assume your assent, since you do not answer. Do we not hold that supernatural beings are either gods or the children of gods? Do you agree or not? d

Certainly.

Then if I believe in supernatural beings, as you assert, if these supernatural beings are gods in any sense, we shall reach the conclusion which I mentioned just now when I said that you were testing my intelligence for your own amusement, by stating first that I do not believe in gods, and then again that I do, since I believe in supernatural beings. If on the other hand these supernatural beings are bastard children of the gods by nymphs or other mothers, as they are reputed to be, who in the world would believe in the children of gods and not in the gods themselves? It would be as ridiculous as to believe in the
e young of horses or donkeys and not in horses and donkeys themselves. No, Meletus, there is no avoiding the conclusion that you brought this charge against me as a test of my wisdom, or else in despair of finding a genuine offense of which to accuse me. As for your prospect of convincing any living person with even a smattering of intelligence that belief in supernatural and divine activities does not imply belief in supernatural and divine beings, and vice versa, it is outside all the
28 bounds of possibility.

As a matter of fact, gentlemen, I do not feel that it requires much defense to clear myself of Meletus' accusation. What I have said already is enough. But you know very well the truth of what I said in an earlier part of my speech, that I have incurred a great deal of bitter hostility, and this is what will bring about my destruction, if anything does—not Meletus nor Anytus, but the slander and jealousy of a very large section of the people. They have been fatal to a great many
b other innocent men, and I suppose will continue to be so; there is no likelihood that they will stop at me. But perhaps someone will say, Do you feel no compunction, Socrates, at having followed a line of action which puts you in danger of the death penalty?

I might fairly reply to him, You are mistaken, my friend, if you think that a man who is worth anything ought to spend his time weighing up the prospects of life and death. He has only one thing to consider in performing any action—that is, whether he is acting rightly or wrongly, like a good man or a bad one. On your view the he-
c roes who died at Troy would be poor creatures, especially the son of Thetis. He, if you remember, made light of danger in comparison with incurring dishonor when his goddess mother warned him, eager as he was to kill Hector, in some such words as these, I fancy: My son, if you avenge your comrade Patroclus' death and kill Hector, you will die yourself—'Next after Hector is thy fate prepared.' When he heard this warning, he made light of his death and danger, being much more
d afraid of an ignoble life and of failing to avenge his friends. 'Let me die forthwith,' said he, 'when I have requited the villain, rather than remain here by the beaked ships to be mocked, a burden on the ground.' [1] Do you suppose that he gave a thought to death and danger?

[1] *Iliad* 18.96 sq.

The truth of the matter is this, gentlemen. Where a man has once taken up his stand, either because it seems best to him or in obedience to his orders, there I believe he is bound to remain and face the danger, taking no account of death or anything else before dishonor.

This being so, it would be shocking inconsistency on my part, gentlemen, if, when the officers whom you chose to command me assigned me my position at Potidaea and Amphipolis and Delium, I remained at my post like anyone else and faced death, and yet afterward, when God appointed me, as I supposed and believed, to the duty of leading the philosophical life, examining myself and others, I were then through fear of death or of any other danger to desert my post. That would indeed be shocking, and then I might really with justice be summoned into court for not believing in the gods, and disobeying the oracle, and being afraid of death, and thinking that I am wise when I am not. For let me tell you, gentlemen, that to be afraid of death is only another form of thinking that one is wise when one is not; it is to think that one knows what one does not know. No one knows with regard to death whether it is not really the greatest blessing that can happen to a man, but people dread it as though they were certain that it is the greatest evil, and this ignorance, which thinks that it knows what it does not, must surely be ignorance most culpable. This, I take it, gentlemen, is the degree, and this the nature of my advantage over the rest of mankind, and if I were to claim to be wiser than my neighbor in any respect, it would be in this—that not possessing any real knowledge of what comes after death, I am also conscious that I do not possess it. But I do know that to do wrong and to disobey my superior, whether God or man, is wicked and dishonorable, and so I shall never feel more fear or aversion for something which, for all I know, may really be a blessing, than for those evils which I know to be evils.

Suppose, then, that you acquit me, and pay no attention to Anytus, who has said that either I should not have appeared before this court at all, or, since I have appeared here, I must be put to death, because if I once escaped your sons would all immediately become utterly demoralized by putting the teaching of Socrates into practice. Suppose that, in view of this, you said to me, Socrates, on this occasion we shall disregard Anytus and acquit you, but only on one condition, that you give up spending your time on this quest and stop philosophizing. If we catch you going on in the same way, you shall be put to death.

Well, supposing, as I said, that you should offer to acquit me on these terms, I should reply, Gentlemen, I am your very grateful and devoted servant, but I owe a greater obedience to God than to you, and so long as I draw breath and have my faculties, I shall never stop practicing philosophy and exhorting you and elucidating the truth for everyone that I meet. I shall go on saying, in my usual way, My very

good friend, you are an Athenian and belong to a city which is the greatest and most famous in the world for its wisdom and strength. Are you not ashamed that you give your attention to acquiring as
e much money as possible, and similarly with reputation and honor, and give no attention or thought to truth and understanding and the perfection of your soul?

And if any of you disputes this and professes to care about these things, I shall not at once let him go or leave him. No, I shall question him and examine him and test him; and if it appears that in spite of his profession he has made no real progress toward goodness, I shall
30 reprove him for neglecting what is of supreme importance, and giving his attention to trivialities. I shall do this to everyone that I meet, young or old, foreigner or fellow citizen, but especially to you, my fellow citizens, inasmuch as you are closer to me in kinship. This, I do assure you, is what my God commands, and it is my belief that no greater good has ever befallen you in this city than my service to my God. For I spend all my time going about trying to persuade you, young and old, to make your first and chief concern not for your bod-
b ies nor for your possessions, but for the highest welfare of your souls, proclaiming as I go, Wealth does not bring goodness, but goodness brings wealth and every other blessing, both to the individual and to the state.

Now if I corrupt the young by this message, the message would seem to be harmful, but if anyone says that my message is different from this, he is talking nonsense. And so, gentlemen, I would say, You can please yourselves whether you listen to Anytus or not, and whether you acquit me or not. You know that I am not going to alter
c my conduct, not even if I have to die a hundred deaths.

Order, please, gentlemen! Remember my request to give me a hearing without interruption. Besides, I believe that it will be to your advantage to listen. I am going to tell you something else, which may provoke a storm of protest, but please restrain yourselves. I assure you that if I am what I claim to be, and you put me to death, you will harm yourselves more than me. Neither Meletus nor Anytus can do me any
d harm at all; they would not have the power, because I do not believe that the law of God permits a better man to be harmed by a worse. No doubt my accuser might put me to death or have me banished or deprived of civic rights, but even if he thinks—as he probably does, and others too, I dare say—that these are great calamities, I do not think so. I believe that it is far worse to do what he is doing now, trying to put an innocent man to death. For this reason, gentlemen, so far from pleading on my own behalf, as might be supposed, I am really pleading on yours, to save you from misusing the gift of God by condemning
e me. If you put me to death, you will not easily find anyone to take my place. It is literally true, even if it sounds rather comical, that God has specially appointed me to this city, as though it were a large thorough-

bred horse which because of its great size is inclined to be lazy and
needs the stimulation of some stinging fly. It seems to me that God
has attached me to this city to perform the office of such a fly, and all
day long I never cease to settle here, there, and everywhere, rousing,
persuading, reproving every one of you. You will not easily find an- 31
other like me, gentlemen, and if you take my advice you will spare
my life. I suspect, however, that before long you will awake from your
drowsing, and in your annoyance you will take Anytus' advice and
finish me off with a single slap, and then you will go on sleeping till
the end of your days, unless God in his care for you sends someone to
take my place.

   If you doubt whether I am really the sort of person who would
have been sent to this city as a gift from God, you can convince your- b
selves by looking at it in this way. Does it seem natural that I should
have neglected my own affairs and endured the humiliation of allowing my family to be neglected for all these years, while I busied myself all the time on your behalf, going like a father or an elder brother
to see each one of you privately, and urging you to set your thoughts
on goodness? If I had got any enjoyment from it, or if I had been paid
for my good advice, there would have been some explanation for my
conduct, but as it is you can see for yourselves that although my accusers unblushingly charge me with all sorts of other crimes, there is
one thing that they have not had the impudence to pretend on any tes- c
timony, and that is that I have ever exacted or asked a fee from anyone. The witness that I can offer to prove the truth of my statement is,
I think, a convincing one—my poverty.

   It may seem curious that I should go round giving advice like this
and busying myself in people's private affairs, and yet never venture
publicly to address you as a whole and advise on matters of state. The
reason for this is what you have often heard me say before on many
other occasions—that I am subject to a divine or supernatural experi- d
ence, which Meletus saw fit to travesty in his indictment. It began
in my early childhood—a sort of voice which comes to me, and when
it comes it always dissuades me from what I am proposing to do, and
never urges me on. It is this that debars me from entering public life,
and a very good thing too, in my opinion, because you may be quite
sure, gentlemen, that if I had tried long ago to engage in politics, I
should long ago have lost my life, without doing any good either to you
or to myself. Please do not be offended if I tell you the truth. No man e
on earth who conscientiously opposes either you or any other organ-
ized democracy, and flatly prevents a great many wrongs and illegali-
ties from taking place in the state to which he belongs, can possibly
escape with his life. The true champion of justice, if he intends to sur- 32
vive even for a short time, must necessarily confine himself to private
life and leave politics alone.

   I will offer you substantial proofs of what I have said—not

theories, but what you can appreciate better, facts. Listen while I describe my actual experiences, so that you may know that I would never
submit wrongly to any authority through fear of death, but would refuse even at the cost of my life. It will be a commonplace story, such
as you often hear in the courts, but it is true.

b   The only office which I have ever held in our city, gentlemen, was
when I was elected to the Council. It so happened that our group was
acting as the executive when you decided that the ten commanders
who had failed to rescue the men who were lost in the naval engage-
ment should be tried en bloc, which was illegal, as you all recognized
later. On this occasion I was the only member of the executive who in-
sisted that you should not act unconstitutionally, and voted against
the proposal; and although your leaders were all ready to denounce
and arrest me, and you were all urging them on at the top of your
c   voices, I thought that it was my duty to face it out on the side of law
and justice rather than support you, through fear of prison or death,
in your wrong decision.

      This happened while we were still under a democracy. When the
oligarchy came into power, the Thirty Commissioners in their turn
summoned me and four others to the Round Chamber and instructed
us to go and fetch Leon of Salamis from his home for execution. This
was of course only one of many instances in which they issued such
instructions, their object being to implicate as many people as possible
in their wickedness. On this occasion, however, I again made it clear
d   not by my words but by my actions that death did not matter to me at
all—if that is not too strong an expression—but that it mattered all
the world to me that I should do nothing wrong or wicked. Powerful
as it was, that government did not terrify me into doing a wrong action. When we came out of the Round Chamber, the other four went
off to Salamis and arrested Leon, and I went home. I should probably
have been put to death for this, if the government had not fallen soon
e   afterward. There are plenty of people who will testify to these statements.

      Do you suppose that I should have lived as long as I have if I had
moved in the sphere of public life, and conducting myself in that
sphere like an honorable man, had always upheld the cause of right,
and conscientiously set this end above all other things? Not by a very
33 long way, gentlemen; neither would any other man. You will find that
throughout my life I have been consistent in any public duties that I
have performed, and the same also in my personal dealings. I have
never countenanced any action that was incompatible with justice on
the part of any person, including those whom some people maliciously
call my pupils. I have never set up as any man's teacher, but if anyone,
young or old, is eager to hear me conversing and carrying out my private mission, I never grudge him the opportunity; nor do I charge a
b   fee for talking to him, and refuse to talk without one. I am ready to

answer questions for rich and poor alike, and I am equally ready if anyone prefers to listen to me and answer my questions. If any given one of these people becomes a good citizen or a bad one, I cannot fairly be held responsible, since I have never promised or imparted any teaching to anybody, and if anyone asserts that he has ever learned or heard from me privately anything which was not open to everyone else, you may be quite sure that he is not telling the truth.

But how is it that some people enjoy spending a great deal of time in my company? You have heard the reason, gentlemen; I told you c quite frankly. It is because they enjoy hearing me examine those who think that they are wise when they are not—an experience which has its amusing side. This duty I have accepted, as I said, in obedience to God's commands given in oracles and dreams and in every other way that any other divine dispensation has ever impressed a duty upon man. This is a true statement, gentlemen, and easy to verify. If it is a fact that I am in process of corrupting some of the young, and have d succeeded already in corrupting others, and if it were a fact that some of the latter, being now grown up, had discovered that I had ever given them bad advice when they were young, surely they ought now to be coming forward to denounce and punish me. And if they did not like to do it themselves, you would expect some of their families—their fathers and brothers and other near relations—to remember it now, if their own flesh and blood had suffered any harm from me. Certainly a great many of them have found their way into this court, as I can see for myself—first Crito over there, my contemporary and near e neighbor, the father of this young man Critobulus, and then Lysanias of Sphettus, the father of Aeschines here, and next Antiphon of Cephisus, over there, the father of Epigenes. Then besides there are all those whose brothers have been members of our circle—Nicostratus, the son of Theozotides, the brother of Theodotus, but Theodotus is dead, so he cannot appeal to his brother, and Paralus here, the son of Demodocus, whose brother was Theages. And here is Adimantus, 34 the son of Ariston, whose brother Plato is over there, and Aeantodorus, whose brother Apollodorus is here on this side. I can name many more besides, some of whom Meletus most certainly ought to have produced as witnesses in the course of his speech. If he forgot to do so then, let him do it now—I am willing to make way for him. Let him state whether he has any such evidence to offer. On the contrary, gentlemen, you will find that they are all prepared to help me—the corrupter and evil genius of their nearest and dearest relatives, as Meletus and Anytus say. The actual victims of my corrupting in- b fluence might perhaps be excused for helping me; but as for the uncorrupted, their relations of mature age, what other reason can they have for helping me except the right and proper one, that they know Meletus is lying and I am telling the truth?

There, gentlemen, that, and perhaps a little more to the same

effect, is the substance of what I can say in my defense. It may be that
c some one of you, remembering his own case, will be annoyed that
whereas he, in standing his trial upon a less serious charge than this,
made pitiful appeals to the jury with floods of tears, and had his in-
fant children produced in court to excite the maximum of sympathy,
and many of his relatives and friends as well, I on the contrary intend to do nothing of the sort, and that, although I am facing, as it
might appear, the utmost danger. It may be that one of you, reflecting
on these facts, will be prejudiced against me, and being irritated by his
reflections, will give his vote in anger. If one of you is so disposed—I
d do not expect it, but there is the possibility—I think that I should be
quite justified in saying to him, My dear sir, of course I have some relatives. To quote the very words of Homer, even I am not sprung 'from
an oak or from a rock,' [2] but from human parents, and consequently I
have relatives—yes, and sons too, gentlemen, three of them, one almost grown up and the other two only children—but all the same I
am not going to produce them here and beseech you to acquit me.

Why do I not intend to do anything of this kind? Not out of per-
e versity, gentlemen, nor out of contempt for you; whether I am brave
or not in the face of death has nothing to do with it. The point is that
for my own credit and yours and for the credit of the state as a whole,
I do not think that it is right for me to use any of these methods at my
age and with my reputation—which may be true or it may be false,
35 but at any rate the view is held that Socrates is different from the
common run of mankind. Now if those of you who are supposed to be
distinguished for wisdom or courage or any other virtue are to behave
in this way, it would be a disgrace. I have often noticed that some people of this type, for all their high standing, go to extraordinary lengths
when they come up for trial, which shows that they think it will be a
dreadful thing to lose their lives—as though they would be immortal
if you did not put them to death! In my opinion these people bring disgrace upon our city. Any of our visitors might be excused for thinking
b that the finest specimens of Athenian manhood, whom their fellow
citizens select on their merits to rule over them and hold other high
positions, are no better than women. If you have even the smallest
reputation, gentlemen, you ought not to descend to these methods;
and if we do so, you must not give us license. On the contrary, you
must make it clear that anyone who stages these pathetic scenes and
so brings ridicule upon our city is far more likely to be condemned
than if he kept perfectly quiet.

But apart from all question of appearances, gentlemen, I do not
c think that it is right for a man to appeal to the jury or to get himself
acquitted by doing so; he ought to inform them of the facts and convince them by argument. The jury does not sit to dispense justice as

[2] *Odyssey* 19.163.

a favor, but to decide where justice lies, and the oath which they have sworn is not to show favor at their own discretion, but to return a just and lawful verdict. It follows that we must not develop in you, nor you allow to grow in yourselves, the habit of perjury; that would be sinful for us both. Therefore you must not expect me, gentlemen, to behave toward you in a way which I consider neither reputable nor moral nor consistent with my religious duty, and above all you must not expect d it when I stand charged with impiety by Meletus here. Surely it is obvious that if I tried to persuade you and prevail upon you by my entreaties to go against your solemn oath, I should be teaching you contempt for religion, and by my very defense I should be accusing myself of having no religious belief. But that is very far from the truth. I have a more sincere belief, gentlemen, than any of my accusers, and I leave it to you and to God to judge me as it shall be best for me and for yourselves.

There are a great many reasons, gentlemen, why I am not dis- e tressed by this result—I mean your condemnation of me—but the 36 chief reason is that the result was not unexpected. What does surprise me is the number of votes cast on the two sides. I should never have believed that it would be such a close thing, but now it seems that if a mere thirty votes had gone the other way, I should have been acquitted. Even as it is, I feel that so far as Meletus' part is concerned I have been acquitted, and not only that, but anyone can see that if Anytus and Lycon had not come forward to accuse me, Meletus would actually have forfeited his one thousand drachmas for not having ob- b tained one fifth of the votes.

However, we must face the fact that he demands the death penalty. Very good. What alternative penalty shall I propose to you, gentlemen? Obviously it must be adequate. Well, what penalty do I deserve to pay or suffer, in view of what I have done?

I have never lived an ordinary quiet life. I did not care for the things that most people care about—making money, having a comfortable home, high military or civil rank, and all the other activities, political appointments, secret societies, party organizations, which go on in our city. I thought that I was really too strict in my principles c to survive if I went in for this sort of thing. So instead of taking a course which would have done no good either to you or to me, I set myself to do you individually in private what I hold to be the greatest possible service. I tried to persuade each one of you not to think more of practical advantages than of his mental and moral well-being, or in general to think more of advantage than of well-being in the case of the state or of anything else. What do I deserve for behaving in this way? Some reward, gentlemen, if I am bound to suggest what I d really deserve, and what is more, a reward which would be appropriate for myself. Well, what is appropriate for a poor man who is a

public benefactor and who requires leisure for giving you moral encouragement? Nothing could be more appropriate for such a person than free maintenance at the state's expense. He deserves it much more than any victor in the races at Olympia, whether he wins with a single horse or a pair or a team of four. These people give you the
e semblance of success, but I give you the reality; they do not need maintenance, but I do. So if I am to suggest an appropriate penalty
37 which is strictly in accordance with justice, I suggest free maintenance by the state.

Perhaps when I say this I may give you the impression, as I did in my remarks about exciting sympathy and making passionate appeals, that I am showing a deliberate perversity. That is not so, gentlemen. The real position is this. I am convinced that I never wrong anyone intentionally, but I cannot convince you of this, because we have had so little time for discussion. If it was your practice, as it is with other
b nations, to give not one day but several to the hearing of capital trials, I believe that you might have been convinced, but under present conditions it is not easy to dispose of grave allegations in a short space of time. So, being convinced that I do no wrong to anybody, I can hardly be expected to wrong myself by asserting that I deserve something bad, or by proposing a corresponding penalty. Why should I? For fear of suffering this penalty proposed by Meletus, when, as I said, I do not know whether it is a good thing or a bad? Do you expect me to choose something which I know very well is bad by making my
c counterproposal? Imprisonment? Why should I spend my days in prison, in subjection to the periodically appointed officers of the law? A fine, with imprisonment until it is paid? In my case the effect would be just the same, because I have no money to pay a fine. Or shall I suggest banishment? You would very likely accept the suggestion.

I should have to be desperately in love with life to do that, gentlemen. I am not so blind that I cannot see that you, my fellow citizens,
d have come to the end of your patience with my discussions and conversations. You have found them too irksome and irritating, and now you are trying to get rid of them. Will any other people find them easy to put up with? That is most unlikely, gentlemen. A fine life I should have if I left this country at my age and spent the rest of my days trying one city after another and being turned out every time! I know very well that wherever I go the young people will listen to my conversation just as they do here, and if I try to keep them off, they will make their elders drive me out, while if I do not, the fathers and
e other relatives will drive me out of their own accord for the sake of the young.

Perhaps someone may say, But surely, Socrates, after you have left us you can spend the rest of your life in quietly minding your own business.

This is the hardest thing of all to make some of you understand.

If I say that this would be disobedience to God, and that is why I cannot 'mind my own business,' you will not believe that I am serious. If
on the other hand I tell you that to let no day pass without discussing 38
goodness and all the other subjects about which you hear me talking
and examining both myself and others is really the very best thing
that a man can do, and that life without this sort of examination is
not worth living, you will be even less inclined to believe me. Nevertheless that is how it is, gentlemen, as I maintain, though it is not easy
to convince you of it. Besides, I am not accustomed to think of myself
as deserving punishment. If I had money, I would have suggested a
fine that I could afford, because that would not have done me any b
harm. As it is, I cannot, because I have none, unless of course you like
to fix the penalty at what I could pay. I suppose I could probably afford a mina. I suggest a fine of that amount.

One moment, gentlemen. Plato here, and Crito and Critobulus
and Apollodorus, want me to propose thirty minas, on their security.
Very well, I agree to this sum, and you can rely upon these gentlemen
for its payment. c

Well, gentlemen, for the sake of a very small gain in time you are
going to earn the reputation—and the blame from those who wish to
disparage our city—of having put Socrates to death, 'that wise man'
—because they will say I am wise even if I am not, these people who
want to find fault with you. If you had waited just a little while, you
would have had your way in the course of nature. You can see that I
am well on in life and near to death. I am saying this not to all of you
but to those who voted for my execution, and I have something else to d
say to them as well.

No doubt you think, gentlemen, that I have been condemned for
lack of the arguments which I could have used if I had thought it right
to leave nothing unsaid or undone to secure my acquittal. But that is
very far from the truth. It is not a lack of arguments that has caused
my condemnation, but a lack of effrontery and impudence, and the
fact that I have refused to address you in the way which would give
you most pleasure. You would have liked to hear me weep and wail,
doing and saying all sorts of things which I regard as unworthy of e
myself, but which you are used to hearing from other people. But I did
not think then that I ought to stoop to servility because I was in danger, and I do not regret now the way in which I pleaded my case. I
would much rather die as the result of this defense than live as the result of the other sort. In a court of law, just as in warfare, neither I nor
any other ought to use his wits to escape death by any means. In battle 39
it is often obvious that you could escape being killed by giving up
your arms and throwing yourself upon the mercy of your pursuers,
and in every kind of danger there are plenty of devices for avoiding
death if you are unscrupulous enough to stick at nothing. But I

suggest, gentlemen, that the difficulty is not so much to escape death; the real difficulty is to escape from doing wrong, which is far more
b fleet of foot. In this present instance I, the slow old man, have been overtaken by the slower of the two, but my accusers, who are clever and quick, have been overtaken by the faster—by iniquity. When I leave this court I shall go away condemned by you to death, but they will go away convicted by truth herself of depravity and wickedness. And they accept their sentence even as I accept mine. No doubt it was bound to be so, and I think that the result is fair enough.

c   Having said so much, I feel moved to prophesy to you who have given your vote against me, for I am now at that point where the gift of prophecy comes most readily to men—at the point of death. I tell you, my executioners, that as soon as I am dead, vengeance shall fall upon you with a punishment far more painful than your killing of me. You have brought about my death in the belief that through it you will be delivered from submitting your conduct to criticism, but I say that the result will be just the opposite. You will have more critics,
d whom up till now I have restrained without your knowing it, and being younger they will be harsher to you and will cause you more annoyance. If you expect to stop denunciation of your wrong way of life by putting people to death, there is something amiss with your reasoning. This way of escape is neither possible nor creditable. The best and easiest way is not to stop the mouths of others, but to make yourselves as good men as you can. This is my last message to you who
e voted for my condemnation.

     As for you who voted for my acquittal, I should very much like to say a few words to reconcile you to the result, while the officials are busy and I am not yet on my way to the place where I must die. I ask you, gentlemen, to spare me these few moments. There is no reason why we should not exchange fancies while the law permits. I look
40 upon you as my friends, and I want you to understand the right way of regarding my present position.

     Gentlemen of the jury—for *you* deserve to be so called—I have had a remarkable experience. In the past the prophetic voice to which I have become accustomed has always been my constant companion, opposing me even in quite trivial things if I was going to take the wrong course. Now something has happened to me, as you can see, which might be thought and is commonly considered to be a supreme
b calamity; yet neither when I left home this morning, nor when I was taking my place here in the court, nor at any point in any part of my speech did the divine sign oppose me. In other discussions it has often checked me in the middle of a sentence, but this time it has never opposed me in any part of this business in anything that I have said or done. What do I suppose to be the explanation? I will tell you. I suspect that this thing that has happened to me is a blessing, and we
c are quite mistaken in supposing death to be an evil. I have good

grounds for thinking this, because my accustomed sign could not have failed to oppose me if what I was doing had not been sure to bring some good result.

We should reflect that there is much reason to hope for a good result on other grounds as well. Death is one of two things. Either it is annihilation, and the dead have no consciousness of anything, or, as we are told, it is really a change—a migration of the soul from this place to another. Now if there is no consciousness but only a dream- d less sleep, death must be a marvelous gain. I suppose that if anyone were told to pick out the night on which he slept so soundly as not even to dream, and then to compare it with all the other nights and days of his life, and then were told to say, after due consideration, how many better and happier days and nights than this he had spent in the course of his life—well, I think that the Great King himself, to e say nothing of any private person, would find these days and nights easy to count in comparison with the rest. If death is like this, then, I call it gain, because the whole of time, if you look at it in this way, can be regarded as no more than one single night. If on the other hand death is a removal from here to some other place, and if what we are told is true, that all the dead are there, what greater blessing could there be than this, gentlemen? If on arrival in the other world, beyond 41 the reach of our so-called justice, one will find there the true judges who are said to preside in those courts, Minos and Rhadamanthus and Aeacus and Triptolemus and all those other half-divinities who were upright in their earthly life, would that be an unrewarding journey? Put it in this way. How much would one of you give to meet Orpheus and Musaeus, Hesiod and Homer? I am willing to die ten times over if this account is true. It would be a specially interesting experience for me to join them there, to meet Palamedes and Ajax, the son of Tel- b amon, and any other heroes of the old days who met their death through an unfair trial, and to compare my fortunes with theirs— it would be rather amusing, I think. And above all I should like to spend my time there, as here, in examining and searching people's minds, to find out who is really wise among them, and who only thinks that he is. What would one not give, gentlemen, to be able to question the leader of that great host against Troy, or Odysseus, or c Sisyphus, or the thousands of other men and women whom one could mention, to talk and mix and argue with whom would be unimaginable happiness? At any rate I presume that they do not put one to death there for such conduct, because apart from the other happiness in which their world surpasses ours, they are now immortal for the rest of time, if what we are told is true.

You too, gentlemen of the jury, must look forward to death with confidence, and fix your minds on this one belief, which is certain —that nothing can harm a good man either in life or after death, and d his fortunes are not a matter of indifference to the gods. This present experience of mine has not come about mechanically. I am quite clear that the time had come when it was better for me to die and be released from my distractions. That is why my sign never turned me back. For my own part I bear no grudge at all against those who condemned me and accused me, although it was not with this kind intention that they did so, but because they thought that they were hurting e me; and that is culpable of them. However, I ask them to grant me one favor. When my sons grow up, gentlemen, if you think that they are putting money or anything else before goodness, take your revenge by plaguing them as I plagued you; and if they fancy themselves for no reason, you must scold them just as I scolded you, for neglecting the important things and thinking that they are good for something 42 when they are good for nothing. If you do this, I shall have had justice at your hands, both I myself and my children.

Now it is time that we were going, I to die and you to live, but which of us has the happier prospect is unknown to anyone but God.

CRITO

Nearly a month elapsed between Socrates' condemnation and execution, a delay not at all in accordance with Athenian custom. The day before the trial, however, a state galley had been sent on a sacred annual mission and until it returned no one could be put to death. For various reasons the mission took much longer than usual, and Socrates' friends used the time to make a plan for getting him out of prison and away from Athens.

The evening before the Crito opens the galley had been sighted, and very early on the following morning Socrates' old and devoted friend, Crito, comes to the prison to lay the plan before him and beseech him to let his friends save him. It will be easy to bribe his jailers. He himself has far more money than will be needed, and there are many others who are eager to contribute. Athens is not the only place where Socrates can live happily. He will find friends wherever he goes.

To this Socrates answers by asking him if it can ever be right to defend oneself against evil by doing evil. Granted that it was unjust to condemn him to death, can it be right for him to escape by breaking the law? What will happen to a state if individual men are able to set aside the laws? A man must always do what his country orders him unless he can change her view of what the law should be.

" 'If you leave the city, Socrates,' the laws argue, 'you shall return wrong for wrong and evil for evil, breaking your agreements and covenants with us, and injuring those whom you least ought to injure —yourself, your friends, your country, and us.'

"That, my dear friend Crito, I do assure you, is what I seem to hear them saying . . . and the sound of their arguments rings so loudly in my head that I cannot hear the other side. However, if you think that you will do any good by it, say what you like."

"Socrates, I have nothing to say."

"Then, Crito, let us follow this course, since God points out the way."

43   SOCRATES: Here already, Crito? Surely it is still early?
CRITO: Indeed it is.
SOCRATES: About what time?
CRITO: Just before dawn.
SOCRATES: I wonder that the warder paid any attention to you.
CRITO: He is used to me now, Socrates, because I come here so often. Besides, he is under some small obligation to me.
SOCRATES: Have you only just come, or have you been here for long?
CRITO: Fairly long.
b   SOCRATES: Then why didn't you wake me at once, instead of sitting by my bed so quietly?
CRITO: I wouldn't dream of such a thing, Socrates. I only wish I were not so sleepless and depressed myself. I have been wondering at you, because I saw how comfortably you were sleeping, and I deliberately didn't wake you because I wanted you to go on being as comfortable as you could. I have often felt before in the course of my life how fortunate you are in your disposition, but I feel it more than ever now in your present misfortune when I see how easily and placidly you put up with it.
SOCRATES: Well, really, Crito, it would be hardly suitable for a
c   man of my age to resent having to die.
CRITO: Other people just as old as you are get involved in these misfortunes, Socrates, but their age doesn't keep them from resenting it when they find themselves in your position.
SOCRATES: Quite true. But tell me, why have you come so early?
CRITO: Because I bring bad news, Socrates—not so bad from your point of view, I suppose, but it will be very hard to bear for me and your other friends, and I think that I shall find it hardest of all.
SOCRATES: Why, what is this news? Has the boat come in
d   from Delos—the boat which ends my reprieve when it arrives?
CRITO: It hasn't actually come in yet, but I expect that it will be here today, judging from the report of some people who have just arrived from Sunium and left it there. It's quite clear from their account that it will be here today, and so by tomorrow, Socrates, you will have to . . . to end your life.
SOCRATES: Well, Crito, I hope that it may be for the best. If the
44 gods will it so, so be it. All the same, I don't think it will arrive today.
CRITO: What makes you think that?
SOCRATES: I will try to explain. I think I am right in saying that I have to die on the day after the boat arrives?

From *The Last Days of Socrates,* translated and with an introduction by Hugh Tredennick (Penguin Classics, Harmondsworth, Middlesex, 1954).

CRITO: That's what the authorities say, at any rate.

SOCRATES: Then I don't think it will arrive on this day that is just beginning, but on the day after. I am going by a dream that I had in the night, only a little while ago. It looks as though you were right not to wake me up.

CRITO: Why, what was the dream about?

SOCRATES: I thought I saw a gloriously beautiful woman dressed in white robes, who came up to me and addressed me in these words: Socrates, 'To the pleasant land of Phthia on the third day thou b shalt come.' [1]

CRITO: Your dream makes no sense, Socrates.

SOCRATES: To my mind, Crito, it is perfectly clear.

CRITO: Too clear, apparently. But look here, Socrates, it is still not too late to take my advice and escape. Your death means a double calamity for me. I shall not only lose a friend whom I can never possibly replace, but besides a great many people who don't know you and me very well will be sure to think that I let you down, because I could have saved you if I had been willing to spend the money. And what c could be more contemptible than to get a name for thinking more of money than of your friends? Most people will never believe that it was you who refused to leave this place although we tried our hardest to persuade you.

SOCRATES: But my dear Crito, why should we pay so much attention to what 'most people' think? The really reasonable people, who have more claim to be considered, will believe that the facts are exactly as they are.

CRITO: You can see for yourself, Socrates, that one has to think d of popular opinion as well. Your present position is quite enough to show that the capacity of ordinary people for causing trouble is not confined to petty annoyances, but has hardly any limits if you once get a bad name with them.

SOCRATES: I only wish that ordinary people *had* an unlimited capacity for doing harm; then they might have an unlimited power for doing good, which would be a splendid thing, if it were so. Actually they have neither. They cannot make a man wise or stupid; they simply act at random.

CRITO: Have it that way if you like, but tell me this, Socrates. I e hope that you aren't worrying about the possible effects on me and the rest of your friends, and thinking that if you escape we shall have trouble with informers for having helped you to get away, and have to forfeit all our property or pay an enormous fine, or even incur some further punishment? If any idea like that is troubling you, you can 45 dismiss it altogether. We are quite entitled to run that risk in saving you, and even worse, if necessary. Take my advice, and be reasonable.

[1] *Iliad* 9.363.

SOCRATES : All that you say is very much in my mind, Crito, and a great deal more besides.

CRITO : Very well, then, don't let it distress you. I know some people who are willing to rescue you from here and get you out of the country for quite a moderate sum. And then surely you realize how cheap these informers are to buy off; we shan't need much money to
b settle them, and I think you've got enough of my money for yourself already. And then even supposing that in your anxiety for my safety you feel that you oughtn't to spend my money, there are these foreign gentlemen staying in Athens who are quite willing to spend theirs. One of them, Simmias of Thebes, has actually brought the money with him for this very purpose, and Cebes and a number of others are quite ready to do the same. So, as I say, you mustn't let any fears on these grounds make you slacken your efforts to escape, and you mustn't feel any misgivings about what you said at your trial—that you wouldn't know what to do with yourself if you left this country. Wherever you go, there are plenty of places where you will find a wel-
c come, and if you choose to go to Thessaly, I have friends there who will make much of you and give you complete protection, so that no one in Thessaly can interfere with you.

Besides, Socrates, I don't even feel that it is right for you to try to do what you are doing, throwing away your life when you might save it. You are doing your best to treat yourself in exactly the same way as your enemies would, or rather did, when they wanted to ruin you. What is more, it seems to me that you are letting your sons down too. You have it in your power to finish their bringing-up and education,
d and instead of that you are proposing to go off and desert them, and so far as you are concerned they will have to take their chance. And what sort of chance are they likely to get? The sort of thing that usually happens to orphans when they lose their parents. Either one ought not to have children at all, or one ought to see their upbringing and education through to the end. It strikes me that you are taking the line of least resistance, whereas you ought to make the choice of a good man and a brave one, considering that you profess to have made goodness your object all through life. Really, I am ashamed, both on
e your account and on ours, your friends'. It will look as though we had played something like a coward's part all through this affair of yours. First there was the way you came into court when it was quite un-necessary—that was the first act. Then there was the conduct of the defense—that was the second. And finally, to complete the farce, we get this situation, which makes it appear that we have let you slip out of our hands through some lack of courage and enterprise on our
46 part, because we didn't save you, and you didn't save yourself, when it would have been quite possible and practicable, if we had been any use at all.

There, Socrates, if you aren't careful, besides the suffering there will be all this disgrace for you and us to bear. Come, make up your mind. Really it's too late for that now; you ought to have it made up already. There is no alternative; the whole thing must be carried through during this coming night. If we lose any more time, it can't be done; it will be too late. I appeal to you, Socrates, on every ground; take my advice and please don't be unreasonable!

SOCRATES: My dear Crito, I appreciate your warm feelings b very much—that is, assuming that they have some justification. If not, the stronger they are, the harder they will be to deal with. Very well, then, we must consider whether we ought to follow your advice or not. You know that this is not a new idea of mine; it has always been my nature never to accept advice from any of my friends unless reflection shows that it is the best course that reason offers. I cannot abandon the principles which I used to hold in the past simply because this accident has happened to me; they seem to me to be much as they were, and I respect and regard the same principles now as be- c fore. So unless we can find better principles on this occasion, you can be quite sure that I shall not agree with you—not even if the power of the people conjures up fresh hordes of bogies to terrify our childish minds, by subjecting us to chains and executions and confiscations of our property.

Well, then, how can we consider the question most reasonably? Suppose that we begin by reverting to this view which you hold about people's opinions. Was it always right to argue that some opinions should be taken seriously but not others? Or was it always wrong? d Perhaps it was right before the question of my death arose, but now we can see clearly that it was a mistaken persistence in a point of view which was really irresponsible nonsense. I should like very much to inquire into this problem, Crito, with your help, and to see whether the argument will appear in any different light to me now that I am in this position, or whether it will remain the same, and whether we shall dismiss it or accept it.

Serious thinkers, I believe, have always held some such view as the one which I mentioned just now, that some of the opinions which people entertain should be respected, and others should not. e Now I ask you, Crito, don't you think that this is a sound principle? You are safe from the prospect of dying tomorrow, in all human probability, and you are not likely to have your judgment upset by this 47 impending calamity. Consider, then, don't you think that this is a sound enough principle, that one should not regard all the opinions that people hold, but only some and not others? What do you say? Isn't that a fair statement?

CRITO: Yes, it is.

SOCRATES: In other words, one should regard the good ones and not the bad?

CRITO: Yes.

SOCRATES : The opinions of the wise being good, and the opinions of the foolish bad?

CRITO : Naturally.

b SOCRATES : To pass on, then, what do you think of the sort of illustration that I used to employ? When a man is in training, and taking it seriously, does he pay attention to all praise and criticism and opinion indiscriminately, or only when it comes from the one qualified person, the actual doctor or trainer?

CRITO : Only when it comes from the one qualified person.

SOCRATES : Then he should be afraid of the criticism and welcome the praise of the one qualified person, but not those of the general public.

CRITO : Obviously.

SOCRATES : So he ought to regulate his actions and exercises and eating and drinking by the judgment of his instructor, who has expert knowledge, rather than by the opinions of the rest of the public.

CRITO : Yes, that is so.

c SOCRATES : Very well. Now if he disobeys the one man and disregards his opinion and commendations, and pays attention to the advice of the many who have no expert knowledge, surely he will suffer some bad effect?

CRITO : Certainly.

SOCRATES : And what is this bad effect? Where is it produced? I mean, in what part of the disobedient person?

CRITO : His body, obviously; that is what suffers.

SOCRATES : Very good. Well now, tell me, Crito—we don't want to go through all the examples one by one—does this apply as a general rule, and above all to the sort of actions which we are trying to decide about, just and unjust, honorable and dishonorable, good and bad? Ought we to be guided and intimidated by the opinion of the

d many or by that of the one—assuming that there is someone with expert knowledge? Is it true that we ought to respect and fear this person more than all the rest put together, and that if we do not follow his guidance we shall spoil and mutilate that part of us which, as we used to say, is improved by right conduct and destroyed by wrong? Or is this all nonsense?

CRITO : No, I think it is true, Socrates.

SOCRATES : Then consider the next step. There is a part of us which is improved by healthy actions and ruined by unhealthy ones.

e If we spoil it by taking the advice of nonexperts, will life be worth living when this part is once ruined? The part I mean is the body. Do you accept this?

CRITO : Yes.

SOCRATES : Well, is life worth living with a body which is worn out and ruined in health?

CRITO : Certainly not.

SOCRATES: What about the part of us which is mutilated by wrong actions and benefited by right ones? Is life worth living with this part ruined? Or do we believe that this part of us, whatever it may be, in which right and wrong operate, is of less importance than 48 the body?

CRITO: Certainly not.

SOCRATES: It is really more precious?

CRITO: Much more.

SOCRATES: In that case, my dear fellow, what we ought to consider is not so much what people in general will say about us but how we stand with the expert in right and wrong, the one authority, who represents the actual truth. So in the first place your proposition is not correct when you say that we should consider popular opinion in questions of what is right and honorable and good, or the opposite. Of course one might object, All the same, the people have the power to put us to death.

CRITO: No doubt about that! Quite true, Socrates. It is a possi- b ble objection.

SOCRATES: But so far as I can see, my dear fellow, the argument which we have just been through is quite unaffected by it. At the same time I should like you to consider whether we are still satisfied on this point, that the really important thing is not to live, but to live well.

CRITO: Why, yes.

SOCRATES: And that to live well means the same thing as to live honorably or rightly?

CRITO: Yes.

SOCRATES: Then in the light of this agreement we must consider whether or not it is right for me to try to get away without an official discharge. If it turns out to be right, we must make the attempt; c if not, we must let it drop. As for the considerations you raise about expense and reputation and bringing up children, I am afraid, Crito, that they represent the reflections of the ordinary public, who put people to death, and would bring them back to life if they could, with equal indifference to reason. Our real duty, I fancy, since the argument leads that way, is to consider one question only, the one which we raised just now. Shall we be acting rightly in paying money and showing gratitude to these people who are going to rescue me, and in escaping or arranging the escape ourselves, or shall we really be act- d ing wrongly in doing all this? If it becomes clear that such conduct is wrong, I cannot help thinking that the question whether we are sure to die, or to suffer any other ill effect for that matter, if we stand our ground and take no action, ought not to weigh with us at all in comparison with the risk of doing what is wrong.

CRITO: I agree with what you say, Socrates, but I wish you would consider what we ought to *do*.

SOCRATES: Let us look at it together, my dear fellow; and if

e you can challenge any of my arguments, do so and I will listen to you;
but if you can't, be a good fellow and stop telling me over and over
again that I ought to leave this place without official permission. I am
very anxious to obtain your approval before I adopt the course which
I have in mind. I don't want to act against your convictions. Now give
your attention to the starting point of this inquiry—I hope that you
will be satisfied with my way of stating it—and try to answer my
49 questions to the best of your judgment.

CRITO: Well, I will try.

SOCRATES: Do we say that one must never willingly do wrong,
or does it depend upon circumstances? Is it true, as we have often
agreed before, that there is no sense in which wrongdoing is good
or honorable? Or have we jettisoned all our former convictions in
these last few days? Can you and I at our age, Crito, have spent all
these years in serious discussions without realizing that we were no
b better than a pair of children? Surely the truth is just what we have
always said. Whatever the popular view is, and whether the alternative is pleasanter than the present one or even harder to bear, the fact
remains that to do wrong is in every sense bad and dishonorable for
the person who does it. Is that our view, or not?

CRITO: Yes, it is.

SOCRATES: Then in no circumstances must one do wrong.

CRITO: No.

SOCRATES: In that case one must not even do wrong when one
is wronged, which most people regard as the natural course.

c CRITO: Apparently not.

SOCRATES: Tell me another thing, Crito. Ought one to do in-
juries or not?

CRITO: Surely not, Socrates.

SOCRATES: And tell me, is it right to do an injury in retaliation,
as most people believe, or not?

CRITO: No, never.

SOCRATES: Because, I suppose, there is no difference between
injuring people and wronging them.

CRITO: Exactly.

SOCRATES: So one ought not to return a wrong or an injury to
d any person, whatever the provocation is. Now be careful, Crito, that
in making these single admissions you do not end by admitting something contrary to your real beliefs. I know that there are and always
will be few people who think like this, and consequently between
those who do think so and those who do not there can be no agreement on principle; they must always feel contempt when they observe
one another's decisions. I want even you to consider very carefully
whether you share my views and agree with me, and whether we can
proceed with our discussion from the established hypothesis that it is
never right to do a wrong or return a wrong or defend oneself against

away wherever he likes. If any of you chooses to go to one of our colonies, supposing that he should not be satisfied with us and the state, or to emigrate to any other country, not one of us laws hinders or prevents him from going away wherever he likes, without any loss of property. On the other hand, if any one of you stands his ground when e he can see how we administer justice and the rest of our public organization, we hold that by so doing he has in fact undertaken to do anything that we tell him. And we maintain that anyone who disobeys is guilty of doing wrong on three separate counts: first because we are his parents, and secondly because we are his guardians, and thirdly because, after promising obedience, he is neither obeying us nor persuading us to change our decision if we are at fault in any way. And although all our orders are in the form of proposals, not of savage 52 commands, and we give him the choice of either persuading us or doing what we say, he is actually doing neither. These are the charges, Socrates, to which we say that you will be liable if you do what you are contemplating, and you will not be the least culpable of your fellow countrymen, but one of the most guilty.

If I asked why, they would no doubt pounce upon me with perfect justice and point out that there are very few people in Athens who have entered into this agreement with them as explicitly as I have. They would say, Socrates, we have substantial evidence that you are b satisfied with us and with the state. You would not have been so exceptionally reluctant to cross the borders of your country if you had not been exceptionally attached to it. You have never left the city to attend a festival or for any other purpose, except on some military expedition. You have never traveled abroad as other people do, and you have never felt the impulse to acquaint yourself with another country or constitution. You have been content with us and with our city. You c have definitely chosen us, and undertaken to observe us in all your activities as a citizen, and as the crowning proof that you are satisfied with our city, you have begotten children in it. Furthermore, even at the time of your trial you could have proposed the penalty of banishment, if you had chosen to do so—that is, you could have done then with the sanction of the state what you are now trying to do without it. But whereas at that time you made a noble show of indifference if you had to die, and in fact preferred death, as you said, to banishment, now you show no respect for your earlier professions, and no regard for us, the laws, whom you are trying to destroy. You are behaving like the lowest type of menial, trying to run away in spite of d the contracts and undertakings by which you agreed to live as a member of our state. Now first answer this question. Are we or are we not speaking the truth when we say that you have undertaken, in deed if not in word, to live your life as a citizen in obedience to us?

What are we to say to that, Crito? Are we not bound to admit it?

CRITO: We cannot help it, Socrates.

SOCRATES: It is a fact, then, they would say, that you are
e breaking covenants and undertakings made with us, although you
made them under no compulsion or misunderstanding, and were not
compelled to decide in a limited time. You had seventy years in which
you could have left the country, if you were not satisfied with us or
felt that the agreements were unfair. You did not choose Sparta or
Crete—your favorite models of good government—or any other Greek
53 or foreign state. You could not have absented yourself from the city
less if you had been lame or blind or decrepit in some other way. It is
quite obvious that you stand by yourself above all other Athenians in
your affection for this city and for us its laws. Who would care for a
city without laws? And now, after all this, are you not going to stand
by your agreement? Yes, you are, Socrates, if you will take our advice,
and then you will at least escape being laughed at for leaving the
city.

We invite you to consider what good you will do to yourself or
your friends if you commit this breach of faith and stain your con-
b science. It is fairly obvious that the risk of being banished and either
losing their citizenship or having their property confiscated will ex-
tend to your friends as well. As for yourself, if you go to one of the
neighboring states, such as Thebes or Megara, which are both well governed, you will enter them as an enemy to their constitution, and all
good patriots will eye you with suspicion as a destroyer of law and order. Incidentally you will confirm the opinion of the jurors who tried
c you that they gave a correct verdict; a destroyer of laws might very
well be supposed to have a destructive influence upon young and foolish human beings. Do you intend, then, to avoid well-governed states
and the higher forms of human society? And if you do, will life be
worth living? Or will you approach these people and have the impudence to converse with them? What arguments will you use, Socrates?
The same which you used here, that goodness and integrity, institu-
tions and laws, are the most precious possessions of mankind? Do you
not think that Socrates and everything about him will appear in a dis-
d reputable light? You certainly ought to think so.

But perhaps you will retire from this part of the world and go to
Crito's friends in Thessaly? That is the home of indiscipline and lax-
ity, and no doubt they would enjoy hearing the amusing story of how
you managed to run away from prison by arraying yourself in some
costume or putting on a shepherd's smock or some other conventional
runaway's disguise, and altering your personal appearance. And will
no one comment on the fact that an old man of your age, probably
with only a short time left to live, should dare to cling so greedily to
e life, at the price of violating the most stringent laws? Perhaps not, if
you avoid irritating anyone. Otherwise, Socrates, you will hear a good
many humiliating comments. So you will live as the toady and slave
of all the populace, literally 'roistering in Thessaly,' as though you had

left this country for Thessaly to attend a banquet there. And where will your discussions about goodness and uprightness be then, we should like to know? But of course you want to live for your chil- 54 dren's sake, so that you may be able to bring them up and educate them. Indeed! By first taking them off to Thessaly and making foreigners of them, so that they may have that additional enjoyment? Or if that is not your intention, supposing that they are brought up here with you still alive, will they be better cared for and educated without you, because of course your friends will look after them? Will they look after your children if you go away to Thessaly, and not if you go away to the next world? Surely if those who profess to be your friends b are worth anything, you must believe that they would care for them.

No, Socrates, be advised by us your guardians, and do not think more of your children or of your life or of anything else than you think of what is right, so that when you enter the next world you may have all this to plead in your defense before the authorities there. It seems clear that if you do this thing, neither you nor any of your friends will be the better for it or be more upright or have a cleaner conscience here in this world, nor will it be better for you when you reach the next. As it is, you will leave this place, when you do, as the victim of a wrong done not by us, the laws, but by your fellow men. c But if you leave in that dishonorable way, returning wrong for wrong and evil for evil, breaking your agreements and covenants with us, and injuring those whom you least ought to injure—yourself, your friends, your country, and us—then you will have to face our anger in your lifetime, and in that place beyond when the laws of the other world know that you have tried, so far as you could, to destroy even us their brothers, they will not receive you with a kindly welcome. Do not take Crito's advice, but follow ours. d

That, my dear friend Crito, I do assure you, is what I seem to hear them saying, just as a mystic seems to hear the strains of music, and the sound of their arguments rings so loudly in my head that I cannot hear the other side. I warn you that, as my opinion stands at present, it will be useless to urge a different view. However, if you think that you will do any good by it, say what you like.

CRITO: No, Socrates, I have nothing to say.

SOCRATES: Then give it up, Crito, and let us follow this course, e since God points out the way.

PHAEDO

Some time after Socrates' death Phaedo, a devoted pupil who had been with him to the end, gives an account of his last hours to a number of his friends.

It was not until evening, he tells them, that Socrates drank the poison. The day had been passed in conversation, as was his way in prison or out, and the talk had turned on the immortality of the soul. Various so-called proofs were discussed, the chief one being that "our birth is but a sleep and a forgetting," that to learn is in part to remember knowledge which must have been gained in another life. In the end, however, this argument is discarded with all the others. Then Socrates brings up a new idea. The soul is immortal because it can perceive, have a share in, truth, goodness, beauty, which are eternal. Man can know God because he has in him something akin to the eternal which cannot die. This is accepted by all present, and Socrates goes on to declare that only in another life can God's justice be shown and to give a lively picture of heaven and hell. But most characteristically he bids his hearers not to accept this description as the truth, and yet "something of the kind must be true."

So the long talk ends. The poison is drunk—one that caused no pain—and does its work. The last words Socrates speaks show better than all the arguments what he believed. As he felt the poison creeping up to his heart he said, "Crito, we ought to offer a cock to Asclepius." It was the Greek custom after recovery from an illness to make an offering to the divine healer, Asclepius. To himself Socrates was recovering, not dying. He was entering not into death, but into life, "life more abundantly."

ECHECRATES: Were you there with Socrates yourself, Phaedo, when he was executed, or did you hear about it from somebody else?

PHAEDO: No, I was there myself, Echecrates.

ECHECRATES: Then what did the master say before he died, and how did he meet his end? I should very much like to know. None of the people in Phlius go to Athens much in these days, and it is a long time since we had any visitor from there who could give us any b definite information, except that he was executed by drinking hemlock. Nobody could tell us anything more than that.

PHAEDO: Then haven't you even heard how his trial went?

ECHECRATES: Yes, someone told us about that, and we were surprised because there was obviously a long interval between it and the execution. How was that, Phaedo?

PHAEDO: A fortunate coincidence, Echecrates. It so happened that on the day before the trial they had just finished garlanding the stern of the ship which Athens sends to Delos.

ECHECRATES: What ship is that?

PHAEDO: The Athenians say that it is the one in which Theseus sailed away to Crete with the seven youths and seven maidens, and saved their lives and his own as well. The story says that the Atheni- b ans made a vow to Apollo that if these young people's lives were saved they would send a solemn mission to Delos every year, and ever since then they have kept their vow to the god, right down to the present day. They have a law that as soon as this mission begins the city must be kept pure, and no public executions may take place until the ship has reached Delos and returned again, which sometimes takes a long time, if the winds happen to hold it back. The mission is con- c sidered to begin as soon as the priest of Apollo has garlanded the stern of the ship, and this happened, as I say, on the day before the trial. That is why Socrates spent such a long time in prison between his trial and execution.

ECHECRATES: But what about the actual circumstances of his death, Phaedo? What was said and done, and which of the master's companions were with him? Or did the authorities refuse them admission, so that he passed away without a friend at his side?

PHAEDO: Oh no, some of them were there—quite a number, d in fact.

ECHECRATES: I wish you would be kind enough to give us a really detailed account—unless you are pressed for time.

PHAEDO: No, not at all. I will try to describe it for you. Nothing gives me more pleasure than recalling the memory of Socrates, either by talking myself or by listening to someone else.

ECHECRATES: Well, Phaedo, you will find that your audience

From *The Last Days of Socrates*, translated and with an introduction by Hugh Tredennick (Penguin Classics, Harmondsworth, Middlesex, 1954).

feels just the same about it. Now try to describe every detail as carefully as you can.

e   PHAEDO: In the first place, my own feelings at the time were quite extraordinary. It never occurred to me to feel sorry for him, as you might have expected me to feel at the deathbed of a very dear friend. The master seemed quite happy, Echecrates, both in his manner and in what he said; he met his death so fearlessly and nobly. I could not help feeling that even on his way to the other world he would be under the providence of God, and that when he arrived there 59 all would be well with him, if it ever has been so with anybody. So I felt no sorrow at all, as you might have expected on such a solemn occasion, and at the same time I felt no pleasure at being occupied in our usual philosophical discussions—that was the form that our conversation took. I felt an absolutely incomprehensible emotion, a sort of curious blend of pleasure and pain combined, as my mind took it in that in a little while my friend was going to die. All of us who were there were affected in much the same way, between laughing and crying; one of us in particular, Apollodorus—you know what b he is like, don't you?

ECHECRATES: Of course I do.

PHAEDO: Well, he quite lost control of himself, and I and the others were very much upset.

ECHECRATES: Who were actually there, Phaedo?

PHAEDO: Why, of the local people there were this man Apollodorus, and Critobulus and his father, and then there were Hermogenes and Epigenes and Aeschines and Antisthenes. Oh yes, and Ctesippus of Paeania, and Menexenus, and some other local people. I believe that Plato was ill.

ECHECRATES: Were there any visitors from outside?

c   PHAEDO: Yes, Simmias of Thebes, with Cebes and Phaedondas, and Euclides and Terpsion from Megara.

ECHECRATES: Why, weren't Aristippus and Cleombrotus there?

PHAEDO: No, they were in Aegina, apparently.

ECHECRATES: Was there anybody else?

PHAEDO: I think that's about all.

ECHECRATES: Well, what form did the discussion take?

PHAEDO: I will try to tell you all about it from the very be- d ginning. We had all made it our regular practice, even in the period before, to visit Socrates every day. We used to meet at daybreak by the courthouse where the trial was held, because it was close to the prison. We always spent some time in conversation while we waited for the door to open, which was never very early, and when it did open, we used to go in to see Socrates, and generally spent the day with him. On this particular day we met earlier than usual, because e when we left the prison on the evening before, we heard that the boat had just arrived back from Delos; so we urged one another to meet at the same place as early as possible. When we arrived, the porter, instead of letting us in as usual, told us to wait and not to come in until he gave us the word. The commissioners are taking off Socrates' chains, he said, and warning him that he is to die today.

After a short interval he came back and told us to go in. When we went inside we found Socrates just released from his chains, and 60 Xanthippe—you know her!—sitting by him with the little boy on her knee. As soon as Xanthippe saw us she broke out into the sort of remark you would expect from a woman, Oh, Socrates, this is the last time that you and your friends will be able to talk together!

Socrates looked at Crito. Crito, he said, someone had better take her home.

Some of Crito's servants led her away crying hysterically. Socrates sat up on the bed and drew up his leg and massaged it, saying as b he did so, What a queer thing it is, my friends, this sensation which is popularly called pleasure! It is remarkable how closely it is connected with its conventional opposite, pain. They will never come to a man both at once, but if you pursue one of them and catch it, you are nearly always compelled to have the other as well; they are like two bodies attached to the same head. I am sure that if Aesop had thought c of it he would have made up a fable about them, something like this— God wanted to stop their continual quarreling, and when he found that it was impossible, he fastened their heads together; so wherever one of them appears, the other is sure to follow after. That is exactly what seems to be happening to me. I had a pain in my leg from the fetter, and now I feel the pleasure coming that follows it.

Here Cebes broke in and said, Oh yes, Socrates, I am glad you reminded me. Evenus asked me a day or two ago, as others have done before, about the lyrics which you have been composing lately by d adapting Aesop's fables and 'The Prelude' to Apollo. He wanted to know what induced you to write them now after you had gone to prison, when you had never done anything of the kind before. If you would like me to be able to answer Evenus when he asks me again— as I am sure he will—tell me what I am to say.

Tell him the truth, said Socrates, that I did not compose them to rival either him or his poetry—which I knew would not be easy. I did e it in the attempt to discover the meaning of certain dreams, and to clear my conscience, in case this was the art which I had been told to practice. It is like this, you see. In the course of my life I have often had the same dream, appearing in different forms at different times, but always saying the same thing, 'Socrates, practice and cultivate the arts.' In the past I used to think that it was impelling and exhorting me to do what I was actually doing; I mean that the dream, like a spectator encouraging a runner in a race, was urging me on to do what I was doing already, that is, practicing the arts, because phi- 61 losophy is the greatest of the arts, and I was practicing it. But ever since my trial, while the festival of the god has been delaying my execution, I have felt that perhaps it might be this popular form of art that the dream intended me to practice, in which case I ought to practice it and not disobey. I thought it would be safer not to take my departure before I had cleared my conscience by writing poetry and so obeying the dream. I began with some verses in honor of the god whose festival it was. When I had finished my hymn, I reflected that a poet, if he is to be worthy of the name, ought to work on imaginative themes, not descriptive ones, and I was not good at inventing stories. So I availed myself of some of Aesop's fables which were ready to hand and familiar to me, and I versified the first of them that suggested themselves. You can tell Evenus this, Cebes, and bid him farewell from me, and tell him, if he is wise, to follow me as quickly as he can. I shall be going today, it seems; those are my country's orders.

What a piece of advice for Evenus, Socrates! said Simmias. I have had a good deal to do with him before now, and from what I know of him he will not be at all ready to obey you.

Why? he asked. Isn't Evenus a philosopher?

So I believe, said Simmias.

Well then, he will be quite willing, just like anyone else who is properly grounded in philosophy. However, he will hardly do himself violence, because they say that it is not legitimate.

As he spoke he lowered his feet to the ground, and sat like this for the rest of the discussion.

Cebes now asked him, Socrates, what do you mean by saying that it is not legitimate to do oneself violence, although a philosopher will be willing to follow a friend who dies?

Why, Cebes, have you and Simmias never heard about these things while you have been with Philolaus?

Nothing definite, Socrates.

Well, even my information is only based on hearsay, but I don't mind at all telling you what I have heard. I suppose that for one who is soon to leave this world there is no more suitable occupation than inquiring into our views about the future life, and trying to imagine what it is like. What else can one do in the time before sunset?

Tell me then, Socrates, what are the grounds for saying that suicide is not legitimate? I have heard it described as wrong before now, as you suggested, both by Philolaus, when he was staying with us, and by others as well, but I have never yet heard any definite explanation for it.

Well, you must not lose heart, he said. Perhaps you will hear one someday. However, no doubt you will feel it strange that this should be the one question that has an unqualified answer—I mean, if it never happens in the case of life and death, as it does in all other connections, that sometimes and for some people death is better than life. And it probably seems strange to you that it should not be right for those to whom death would be an advantage to benefit themselves, but that they should have to await the services of someone else.

Cebes laughed gently and, dropping into his own dialect, said, Aye, that it does.

Yes, went on Socrates, put in that way it certainly might seem b unreasonable, though perhaps it has some justification. The allegory which the mystics tell us—that we men are put in a sort of guard post, from which one must not release oneself or run away—seems to me to be a high doctrine with difficult implications. All the same, Cebes, I believe that this much is true, that the gods are our keepers, and we men are one of their possessions. Don't you think so?

Yes, I do, said Cebes.

Then take your own case. If one of your possessions were to de- c stroy itself without intimation from you that you wanted it to die, wouldn't you be angry with it and punish it, if you had any means of doing so?

Certainly.

So if you look at it in this way I suppose it is not unreasonable to say that we must not put an end to ourselves until God sends some compulsion like the one which we are facing now.

That seems likely, I admit, said Cebes. But what you were saying just now, that philosophers would be readily willing to die—that seems illogical, Socrates, assuming that we were right in saying a moment ago that God is our keeper and we are his possessions. If this d service is directed by the gods, who are the very best of masters, it is inexplicable that the very wisest of men should not be grieved at quitting it, because he surely cannot expect to provide for himself any better when he is free. On the other hand a stupid person might get the idea that it would be to his advantage to escape from his master. He might not reason it out that one should not escape from a good e master, but remain with him as long as possible, and so he might run away unreflectingly. A sensible man would wish to remain always with his superior. If you look at it in this way, Socrates, the probable thing is just the opposite of what we said just now. It is natural for the wise to be grieved when they die, and for fools to be happy.

When Socrates had listened to this he seemed to me to be amused 63 at Cebes' persistence, and looking round at us he said, You know, Cebes is always investigating arguments, and he is not at all willing to accept every statement at its face value.

Simmias said, Well, but, Socrates, I think that this time there is something in what he says. Why should a really wise man want to desert masters who are better than himself, and to get rid of them so lightly? I think Cebes is aiming his criticism at you, because you are making so light of leaving us, and the gods too, who as you admit are good masters.

What you and Cebes say is perfectly fair, said Socrates. You b mean, I suppose, that I must make a formal defense against this charge.

Exactly, said Simmias.

Very well then, let me try to make a more convincing defense to you than I made at my trial. If I did not expect to enter the company, first, of other wise and good gods, and secondly of men now dead who are better than those who are in this world now, it is true that I should be wrong in not grieving at death. As it is, you can be assured that I

c expect to find myself among good men. I would not insist particularly on this point, but on the other I assure you that I shall insist most strongly—that I shall find there divine masters who are supremely good. That is why I am not so much distressed as I might be, and why I have a firm hope that there is something in store for those who have died, and, as we have been told for many years, something much better for the good than for the wicked.

Well, what is your idea, Socrates? asked Simmias. Do you mean to keep this knowledge to yourself now that you are leaving us, or will you communicate it to us too? I think that we ought to have a share in

d this comfort; besides, it will serve as your defense, if we are satisfied with what you say.

Very well, I will try, he replied. But before I begin, Crito here seems to have been wanting to say something for some time. Let us find out what it is.

Only this, Socrates, said Crito, that the man who is to give you the poison has been asking me for a long time to tell you to talk as little as possible. He says that talking makes you heated, and that you ought not to do anything to affect the action of the poison. Otherwise

e it is sometimes necessary to take a second dose, or even a third.

That is his affair, said Socrates. Let him make his own preparations for administering it twice or three times if necessary.

I was pretty sure you would say that, said Crito, but he's been bothering me for a long time.

Never mind him, said Socrates. Now for you, my jury. I want to explain to you how it seems to me natural that a man who has really devoted his life to philosophy should be cheerful in the face of death,

64 and confident of finding the greatest blessing in the next world when his life is finished. I will try to make clear to you, Simmias and Cebes, how this can be so.

Ordinary people seem not to realize that those who really apply themselves in the right way to philosophy are directly and of their own accord preparing themselves for dying and death. If this is true, and they have actually been looking forward to death all their lives, it would of course be absurd to be troubled when the thing comes for which they have so long been preparing and looking forward.

Simmias laughed and said, Upon my word, Socrates, you have

b made me laugh, though I was not at all in the mood for it. I am sure that if they heard what you said, most people would think—and our fellow countrymen would heartily agree—that it was a very good hit at the philosophers to say that they are half dead already, and that they, the normal people, are quite aware that death would serve the philosophers right.

And they would be quite correct, Simmias—except in thinking that they are 'quite aware.' They are not at all aware in what sense true philosophers are half dead, or in what sense they deserve death, or what sort of death they deserve. But let us dismiss them and talk c among ourselves. Do we believe that there is such a thing as death?

Most certainly, said Simmias, taking up the role of answering.

Is it simply the release of the soul from the body? Is death nothing more or less than this, the separate condition of the body by itself when it is released from the soul, and the separate condition by itself of the soul when released from the body? Is death anything else than this?

No, just that.

Well then, my boy, see whether you agree with me. I fancy that this will help us to find out the answer to our problem. Do you think d that it is right for a philosopher to concern himself with the so-called pleasures connected with food and drink?

Certainly not, Socrates, said Simmias.

What about sexual pleasures?

No, not at all.

And what about the other attentions that we pay to our bodies? Do you think that a philosopher attaches any importance to them? I mean things like providing himself with smart clothes and shoes and other bodily ornaments; do you think that he values them or despises them—in so far as there is no real necessity for him to go in for that sort of thing? e

I think the true philosopher despises them, he said.

Then it is your opinion in general that a man of this kind is not concerned with the body, but keeps his attention directed as much as he can away from it and toward the soul?

Yes, it is.

So it is clear first of all in the case of physical pleasures that the philosopher frees his soul from association with the body, so far as is 65 possible, to a greater extent than other men?

It seems so.

And most people think, do they not, Simmias, that a man who finds no pleasure and takes no part in these things does not deserve to live, and that anyone who thinks nothing of physical pleasures has one foot in the grave?

That is perfectly true.

Now take the acquisition of knowledge. Is the body a hindrance or not, if one takes it into partnership to share an investigation?

What I mean is this. Is there any certainty in human sight and
b hearing, or is it true, as the poets are always dinning into our ears,
that we neither hear nor see anything accurately? Yet if these senses
are not clear and accurate, the rest can hardly be so, because they are
all inferior to the first two. Don't you agree?

Certainly.

Then when is it that the soul attains to truth? When it tries to investigate anything with the help of the body, it is obviously led astray.
c   Quite so.

Is it not in the course of reflection, if at all, that the soul gets a
clear view of facts?

Yes.

Surely the soul can best reflect when it is free of all distractions such as hearing or sight or pain or pleasure of any kind—that
is, when it ignores the body and becomes as far as possible independent, avoiding all physical contacts and associations as much as it
can, in its search for reality.

That is so.

Then here too—in despising the body and avoiding it, and en-
d deavoring to become independent—the philosopher's soul is ahead of
all the rest.

It seems so.

Here are some more questions, Simmias. Do we recognize such a
thing as absolute uprightness?

Indeed we do.

And absolute beauty and goodness too?

Of course.

Have you ever seen any of these things with your eyes?

Certainly not, said he.

Well, have you ever apprehended them with any other bodily
sense? By 'them' I mean not only absolute tallness or health or
strength, but the real nature of any given thing—what it actually is.
e Is it through the body that we get the truest perception of them?
Isn't it true that in any inquiry you are likely to attain more nearly to
knowledge of your object in proportion to the care and accuracy
with which you have prepared yourself to understand that object in itself?

Certainly.

Don't you think that the person who is likely to succeed in this
attempt most perfectly is the one who approaches each object, as far
as possible, with the unaided intellect, without taking account of any
66 sense of sight in his thinking, or dragging any other sense into his
reckoning—the man who pursues the truth by applying his pure and
unadulterated thought to the pure and unadulterated object, cutting
himself off as much as possible from his eyes and ears and virtually all
the rest of his body, as an impediment which by its presence prevents

the soul from attaining to truth and clear thinking? Is not this the person, Simmias, who will reach the goal of reality, if anybody can?

What you say is absolutely true, Socrates, said Simmias.

All these considerations, said Socrates, must surely prompt b serious philosophers to review the position in some such way as this. It looks as though this were a bypath leading to the right track. So long as we keep to the body and our soul is contaminated with this imperfection, there is no chance of our ever attaining satisfactorily to our object, which we assert to be truth. In the first place, the body provides us with innumerable distractions in the pursuit of our necessary sustenance, and any diseases which attack us hinder our quest c for reality. Besides, the body fills us with loves and desires and fears and all sorts of fancies and a great deal of nonsense, with the result that we literally never get an opportunity to think at all about anything. Wars and revolutions and battles are due simply and solely to the body and its desires. All wars are undertaken for the acquisition of wealth, and the reason why we have to acquire wealth is the body, because we are slaves in its service. That is why, on all these ac- d counts, we have so little time for philosophy. Worst of all, if we do obtain any leisure from the body's claims and turn to some line of inquiry, the body intrudes once more into our investigations, interrupting, disturbing, distracting, and preventing us from getting a glimpse of the truth. We are in fact convinced that if we are ever to have pure knowledge of anything, we must get rid of the body and contemplate things by themselves with the soul by itself. It seems, to e judge from the argument, that the wisdom which we desire and upon which we profess to have set our hearts will be attainable only when we are dead, and not in our lifetime. If no pure knowledge is possible in the company of the body, then either it is totally impossible to acquire knowledge, or it is only possible after death, because it is only then that the soul will be separate and independent of 67 the body. It seems that so long as we are alive, we shall continue closest to knowledge if we avoid as much as we can all contact and association with the body, except when they are absolutely necessary, and instead of allowing ourselves to become infected with its nature, purify ourselves from it until God himself gives us deliverance. In this way, by keeping ourselves uncontaminated by the follies of the body, we shall probably reach the company of others like ourselves and gain direct knowledge of all that is pure and uncontaminated b —that is, presumably, of truth. For one who is not pure himself to attain to the realm of purity would no doubt be a breach of universal justice.

Something to this effect, Simmias, is what I imagine all real lovers of learning must think themselves and say to one another. Don't you agree with me?

Most emphatically, Socrates.

Very well, then, said Socrates, if this is true, there is good reason for anyone who reaches the end of this journey which lies before me to hope that there, if anywhere, he will attain the object to which all our efforts have been directed during my past life. So this journey

c which is now ordained for me carries a happy prospect for any other man also who believes that his mind has been prepared by purification.

It does indeed, said Simmias.

And purification, as we saw some time ago in our discussion, consists in separating the soul as much as possible from the body, and accustoming it to withdraw from all contact with the body and con-

d centrate itself by itself, and to have its dwelling, so far as it can, both now and in the future, alone by itself, freed from the shackles of the body. Does not that follow?

Yes, it does, said Simmias.

Is not what we call death a freeing and separation of soul from body?

Certainly, he said.

And the desire to free the soul is found chiefly, or rather only, in the true philosopher. In fact the philosopher's occupation consists precisely in the freeing and separation of soul from body. Isn't that so?

Apparently.

Well then, as I said at the beginning, if a man has trained him-

e self throughout his life to live in a state as close as possible to death, would it not be ridiculous for him to be distressed when death comes to him?

It would, of course.

Then it is a fact, Simmias, that true philosophers make dying their profession, and that to them of all men death is least alarming. Look at it in this way. If they are thoroughly dissatisfied with the body, and long to have their souls independent of it, when this happens would it not be entirely unreasonable to be frightened and distressed? Would they not naturally be glad to set out for the place where there is a prospect of attaining the object of their lifelong desire

68 —which is wisdom—and of escaping from an unwelcome association? Surely there are many who have chosen of their own free will to follow dead lovers and wives and sons to the next world, in the hope of seeing and meeting there the persons whom they loved. If this is so, will a true lover of wisdom who has firmly grasped this same conviction—that he will never attain to wisdom worthy of the name else-

b where than in the next world—will he be grieved at dying? Will he not be glad to make that journey? We must suppose so, my dear boy, that is, if he is a real philosopher, because then he will be of the firm belief that he will never find wisdom in all its purity in any other place. If this is so, would it not be quite unreasonable, as I said just now, for such a man to be afraid of death?

It would, indeed.

So if you see anyone distressed at the prospect of dying, said Socrates, it will be proof enough that he is a lover not of wisdom but of the body. As a matter of fact, I suppose he is also a lover of wealth c and reputation—one or the other, or both.

Yes, you are quite right.

Doesn't it follow, Simmias, he went on, that the virtue which we call courage belongs primarily to the philosophical disposition?

Yes, no doubt it does, he said.

Self-control, too, as it is understood even in the popular sense— not being carried away by the desires, but preserving a decent indifference toward them—is not this appropriate only to those who regard the body with the greatest indifference and spend their lives in philosophy?

Certainly, he said.   d

If you care to consider courage and self-control as practiced by other people, said Socrates, you will find them illogical.

How so, Socrates?

You know, don't you, that everyone except the philosopher regards death as a great evil?

Yes, indeed.

Isn't it true that when a brave man faces death he does so through fear of something worse?

Yes, it is true.

So in everyone except the philosopher courage is due to fear and dread, although it is illogical that fear and cowardice should make a man brave.

Quite so.   e

What about temperate people? Is it not, in just the same way, a sort of self-indulgence that makes them self-controlled? We may say that this is impossible, but all the same those who practice this simple form of self-control are in much the same case as that which I have just described. They are afraid of losing other pleasures which they desire, so they refrain from one kind because they cannot resist the other. Although they define self-indulgence as the condition of being ruled by pleasure, it is really because they cannot resist some 69 pleasures that they succeed in resisting others, which amounts to what I said just now—that they control themselves, in a sense, by self-indulgence.

Yes, that seems to be true.

I congratulate you on your perception, Simmias. No, I am afraid that, from the moral standpoint, it is not the right method to exchange one degree of pleasure or pain or fear for another, like coins of different values. There is only one currency for which all these tokens of ours should be exchanged, and that is wisdom. In fact, it is wisdom that makes possible courage and self-control and integrity or, b

in a word, true goodness, and the presence or absence of pleasures
and fears and other such feelings makes no difference at all, whereas
a system of morality which is based on relative emotional values is a
mere illusion, a thoroughly vulgar conception which has nothing
sound in it and nothing true. The true moral ideal, whether self-control or integrity or courage, is really a kind of purgation from all
c emotions, and wisdom itself is a sort of purification. Perhaps these
people who direct the religious initiations are not so far from the
mark, and all the time there has been an allegorical meaning beneath
their doctrine that he who enters the next world uninitiated and un-
enlightened shall lie in the mire, but he who arrives there purified and
enlightened shall dwell among the gods. You know how the initi-
d ation practitioners say, 'Many bear the emblems, but the devotees are
few'? Well, in my opinion these devotees are simply those who have
lived the philosophical life in the right way—a company which, all
through my life, I have done my best in every way to join, leaving
nothing undone which I could do to attain this end. Whether I was
right in this ambition, and whether we have achieved anything, we
shall know for certain, if God wills, when we reach the other world,
and that, I imagine, will be fairly soon.

This is the defense which I offer you, Simmias and Cebes, to
show that it is natural for me to leave you and my earthly rulers
e without any feeling of grief or bitterness, since I believe that I shall
find there, no less than here, good rulers and good friends. If I am any
more convincing in my defense to you than I was to my Athenian
jury, I shall be satisfied.

When Socrates had finished, Cebes made his reply. The rest of
70 your statement, Socrates, he said, seems excellent to me, but what
you said about the soul leaves the average person with grave misgivings that when it is released from the body it may no longer exist
anywhere, but may be dispersed and destroyed on the very day that
the man himself dies, as soon as it is freed from the body, that as it
emerges it may be dissipated like breath or smoke, and vanish away,
so that nothing is left of it anywhere. Of course if it still existed as an
independent unity, released from all the evils which you have just
described, there would be a strong and glorious hope, Socrates, that
b what you say is true. But I fancy that it requires no little faith and
assurance to believe that the soul exists after death and retains some
active force and intelligence.

Quite true, Cebes, said Socrates. But what are we to do about it?
Is it your wish that we should go on speculating about the subject, to
see whether this view is likely to be true or not?

For my part, said Cebes, I should be very glad to hear what you
think about it.

At any rate, said Socrates, I hardly think that anyone who heard
c us now—even a comic poet—would say that I am wasting time and

discoursing on subjects which do not concern me. So if that is how you feel, we had better continue our inquiry. Let us approach it from this point of view. Do the souls of the departed exist in another world or not?

There is an old legend, which we still remember, to the effect that they *do* exist there, after leaving here, and that they return again to this world and come into being from the dead. If this is so—that the living come into being again from the dead—does it not follow that d our souls exist in the other world? They could not come into being again if they did not exist, and it will be sufficient proof that my contention is true if it really becomes apparent that the living come from the dead, and from nowhere else. But if this is not so, we shall need some other argument.

Quite so, said Cebes.

If you want to understand the question more readily, said Socrates, consider it with reference not only to human beings but to all animals and plants. Let us see whether in general everything that admits of generation is generated in this way and no other—opposites e from opposites, wherever there is an opposite—as for instance beauty is opposite to ugliness and right to wrong, and there are countless other examples. Let us consider whether it is a necessary law that everything which has an opposite is generated from that opposite and from no other source. For example, when a thing becomes bigger, it must, I suppose, have been smaller first before it became bigger?

Yes.

And similarly if it becomes smaller, it must be bigger first, and become smaller afterward?   71

That is so, said Cebes.

And the weaker comes from the stronger, and the faster from the slower?

Certainly.

One more instance. If a thing becomes worse, is it not from being better? And if more just, from being more unjust?

Of course.

Are we satisfied, then, said Socrates, that everything is generated in this way—opposites from opposites?

Perfectly.

Here is another question. Do not these examples present another feature, that between each pair of opposites there are two processes of generation, one from the first to the second, and another from the b second to the first? Between a larger and a smaller object are there not the processes of increase and decrease, and do we not describe them in this way as increasing and decreasing?

Yes, said Cebes.

Is it not the same with separating and combining, cooling and heating, and all the rest of them? Even if we sometimes do not use the actual terms, must it not in fact hold good universally that they come one from the other, and that there is a process of generation from each to the other?

Certainly, said Cebes.

c   Well then, said Socrates, is there an opposite to living, as sleeping is opposite to waking?

Certainly.

What?

Being dead.

So if they are opposites, they come from one another, and have their two processes of generation between the two of them?

Of course.

Very well, then, said Socrates, I will state one pair of opposites which I mentioned just now—the opposites themselves and the processes between them—and you shall state the other. My opposites are sleeping and waking, and I say that waking comes from sleeping and
d sleeping from waking, and that the processes between them are going to sleep and waking up. Does that satisfy you, he asked, or not?

Perfectly.

Now you tell me in the same way, he went on, about life and death. Do you not admit that death is the opposite of life?

I do.

And that they come from one another?

Yes.

Then what comes from the living?

The dead.

And what, asked Socrates, comes from the dead?

I must admit, he said, that it is the living.

So it is from the dead, Cebes, that living things and people come?
e   Evidently.

Then our souls do exist in the next world.

So it seems.

And one of the two processes in this case is really quite certain—dying is certain enough, isn't it?

Yes, it is, said Cebes.

What shall we do, then? Shall we omit the complementary process, and leave a defect here in the law of nature? Or must we supply an opposite process to that of dying?

Surely we must supply it, he said.

And what is it?

Coming to life again.

Then if there is such a thing as coming to life again, said Soc-
72 rates, it must be a process from death to life?

Quite so.

So we agree upon this too—that the living have come from the dead no less than the dead from the living. But I think we decided that if this was so, it was a sufficient proof that the souls of the dead must exist in some place from which they are reborn.

It seems to me, Socrates, he said, that this follows necessarily from our agreement.

I think there is another way too, Cebes, in which you can see that we were not wrong in our agreement. If there were not a constant correspondence in the process of generation between the two sets of opposites, going round in a sort of cycle, if generation were a straight b path to the opposite extreme without any return to the starting point or any deflection, do you realize that in the end everything would have the same quality and reach the same state, and change would cease altogether?

What do you mean?

Nothing difficult to understand, replied Socrates. For example, if 'falling asleep' existed, and 'waking up' did not balance it by making something come out of sleep, you must realize that in the end everything would make Endymion look foolish. He would be nowhere, because the whole world would be in the same state—asleep. And if c everything were combined and nothing separated, we should soon have Anaxagoras' 'all things together.' In just the same way, my dear Cebes, if everything that has some share of life were to die, and if after death the dead remained in that form and did not come to life again, would it not be quite inevitable that in the end everything should be dead and nothing alive? If living things came from other living things, and the living things died, what possible means could d prevent their number from being exhausted by death?

None that I can see, Socrates, said Cebes. What you say seems to be perfectly true.

Yes, Cebes, he said, if anything is true, I believe that this is, and we were not mistaken in our agreement upon it. Coming to life again is a fact, and it is a fact that the living come from the dead, and a fact that the souls of the dead exist.   e

Besides, Socrates, rejoined Cebes, there is that theory which you have often described to us—that what we call learning is really just recollection. If that is true, then surely what we recollect now we must have learned at some time before, which is impossible unless our souls existed somewhere before they entered this human shape. So in that way too it seems likely that the soul is immortal.   73

How did the proofs of that theory go, Cebes? broke in Simmias. Remind me, because at the moment I can't quite remember.

One very good argument, said Cebes, is that when people are asked questions, if the question is put in the right way they can give a perfectly correct answer, which they could not possibly do unless they had some knowledge and a proper grasp of the subject. And then if you confront people with a diagram or anything like that, the way b in which they react is an unmistakable proof that the theory is correct.

And if you don't find that convincing, Simmias, said Socrates, see whether this appeals to you. I suppose that you find it hard to understand how what we call learning can be recollection?

Not at all, said Simmias. All that I want is to be helped to do what we are talking about—to recollect. I can practically remember enough to satisfy me already, from Cebes' approach to the subject, but I should be nonetheless glad to hear how you meant to approach it.

c   I look at it in this way, said Socrates. We are agreed, I suppose, that if a person is to be reminded of anything, he must first know it at some time or other?

Quite so.

Are we also agreed in calling it recollection when knowledge comes in a particular way? I will explain what I mean. Suppose that a person on seeing or hearing or otherwise noticing one thing not only becomes conscious of that thing but also thinks of a something else which is an object of a different sort of knowledge. Are we not justified

d in saying that he was reminded of the object which he thought of?

What do you mean?

Let me give you an example. A human being and a musical instrument, I suppose you will agree, are different objects of knowledge.

Yes, certainly.

Well, you know what happens to lovers when they see a musical instrument or a piece of clothing or any other private property of the person whom they love. When they recognize the thing, their minds conjure up a picture of its owner. That is recollection. In the same way the sight of Simmias often reminds one of Cebes, and of course there are thousands of other examples.

Yes, of course there are, said Simmias.

e   So by recollection we mean the sort of experience which I have just described, especially when it happens with reference to things which we had not seen for such a long time that we had forgotten them.

Quite so.

Well, then, is it possible for a person who sees a picture of a horse or a musical instrument to be reminded of a person, or for someone who sees a picture of Simmias to be reminded of Cebes?

Perfectly.

And is it possible for someone who sees a portrait of Simmias to be reminded of Simmias himself?

74   Yes, it is.

Does it not follow from all this that recollection may be caused either by similar or by dissimilar objects?

Yes, it does.

When you are reminded by similarity, surely you must also be conscious whether the similarity is perfect or only partial.

Yes, you must.

Here is a further step, said Socrates. We admit, I suppose, that there is such a thing as equality—not the equality of stick to stick and stone to stone, and so on, but something beyond all that and distinct from it—absolute equality. Are we to admit this or not?

Yes indeed, said Simmias, most emphatically.   b

And do we know what it is?

Certainly.

Where did we get our knowledge? Was it not from the particular examples that we mentioned just now? Was it not from seeing equal sticks or stones or other equal objects that we got the notion of equality, although it is something quite distinct from them? Look at it in this way. Is it not true that equal stones and sticks sometimes, without changing in themselves, appear equal to one person and unequal to another?

Certainly.

Well, now, have you ever thought that things which were abso-   c lutely equal were unequal, or that equality was inequality?

No, never, Socrates.

Then these equal things are not the same as absolute equality.

Not in the least, as I see it, Socrates.

And yet it is these equal things that have suggested and conveyed to you your knowledge of absolute equality, although they are distinct from it?

Perfectly true.

Whether it is similar to them or dissimilar?

Certainly.

It makes no difference, said Socrates. So long as the sight of one thing suggests another to you, it must be a cause of recollection,   d whether the two things are alike or not.

Quite so.

Well, now, he said, what do we find in the case of the equal sticks and other things of which we were speaking just now? Do they seem to us to be equal in the sense of absolute equality, or do they fall short of it in so far as they only approximate to equality? Or don't they fall short at all?

They do, said Simmias, a long way.

Suppose that when you see something you say to yourself, This thing which I can see has a tendency to be like something else, but it falls short and cannot be really like it, only a poor imitation. Don't   e you agree with me that anyone who receives that impression must in fact have previous knowledge of that thing which he says that the other resembles, but inadequately?

Certainly he must.

Very well, then, is that our position with regard to equal things and absolute equality?

Exactly.

75 Then we must have had some previous knowledge of equality before the time when we first saw equal things and realized that they were striving after equality, but fell short of it.

That is so.

And at the same time we are agreed also upon this point, that we have not and could not have acquired this notion of equality except by sight or touch or one of the other senses. I am treating them as being all the same.

They are the same, Socrates, for the purpose of our argument.

So it must be through the senses that we obtained the notion that all sensible equals are striving after absolute equality but fallb ing short of it. Is that correct?

Yes, it is.

So before we began to see and hear and use our other senses we must somewhere have acquired the knowledge that there is such a thing as absolute equality. Otherwise we could never have realized, by using it as a standard for comparison, that all equal objects of sense are desirous of being like it, but are only imperfect copies.

That is the logical conclusion, Socrates.

Did we not begin to see and hear and possess our other senses from the moment of birth?

Certainly.

c But we admitted that we must have obtained our knowledge of equality before we obtained them.

Yes.

So we must have obtained it before birth.

So it seems.

Then if we obtained it before our birth, and possessed it when we were born, we had knowledge, both before and at the moment of birth, not only of equality and relative magnitudes, but of all absolute standards. Our present argument applies no more to equality than it d does to absolute beauty, goodness, uprightness, holiness, and, as I maintain, all those characteristics which we designate in our discussions by the term 'absolute.' So we must have obtained knowledge of all these characteristics before our birth.

That is so.

And unless we invariably forget it after obtaining it we must always be born *knowing* and continue to *know* all through our lives, because 'to know' means simply to retain the knowledge which one has acquired, and not to lose it. Is not what we call 'forgetting' simply the loss of knowledge, Simmias?

e Most certainly, Socrates.

And if it is true that we acquired our knowledge before our birth, and lost it at the moment of birth, but afterward, by the exercise of our senses upon sensible objects, recover the knowledge which we had once before, I suppose that what we call learning will be the recovery of our own knowledge, and surely we should be right in calling this recollection.

Quite so.

Yes, because we saw that it is possible for the perception of an 76 object by sight or hearing or any of the other senses to suggest to the percipient, through association, whether there is any similarity or not, another object which he has forgotten. So, as I maintain, there are two alternatives. Either we are all born with knowledge of these standards, and retain it throughout our lives, or else, when we speak of people learning, they are simply recollecting what they knew before. In other words, learning is recollection.

Yes, that must be so, Socrates.

Which do you choose, then, Simmias? That we are born with knowledge, or that we recollect after we are born the things of which b we possessed knowledge before we were born?

I don't know which to choose on the spur of the moment, Socrates.

Well, here is another choice for you to make. What do you think about this? Can a person who knows a subject thoroughly explain what he knows?

Most certainly he can.

Do you think that everyone can explain these questions about which we have just been talking?

I should like to think so, said Simmias, but I am very much afraid that by this time tomorrow there will be no one on this earth who can do it properly.

So you don't think, Simmias, that everyone has knowledge about c them?

Far from it.

Then they just recollect what they once learned.

That must be the right answer.

When do our souls acquire this knowledge? It cannot be after the beginning of our mortal life.

No, of course not.

Then it must be before.

Yes.

Then our souls had a previous existence, Simmias, before they took on this human shape. They were independent of our bodies, and they were possessed of intelligence.

Unless perhaps it is at the moment of birth that we acquire knowledge of these things, Socrates. There is still that time available.

No doubt, my dear fellow, but just tell me, what other time is d there to lose it in? We have just agreed that we do not possess it when we are born. Do we lose it at the same moment that we acquire it? Or can you suggest any other time?

No, of course not, Socrates. I didn't realize what nonsense I was talking.

Well, how do we stand now, Simmias? If all these absolute realities, such as beauty and goodness, which we are always talking about, really exist, if it is to them, as we rediscover our own former knowledge of them, that we refer, as copies to their patterns, all the objects
e of our physical perception—if these realities exist, does it not follow that our souls must exist too even before our birth, whereas if they do not exist, our discussion would seem to be a waste of time? Is this the position, that it is logically just as certain that our souls exist before our birth as it is that these realities exist, and that if the one is impossible, so is the other?

It is perfectly obvious to me, Socrates, said Simmias, that the same logical necessity applies to both. It suits me very well that your
77 argument should rely upon the point that our soul's existence before our birth stands or falls with the existence of your grade of reality. I cannot imagine anything more self-evident than the fact that absolute beauty and goodness and all the rest that you mentioned just now exist in the fullest possible sense. In my opinion the proof is quite satisfactory.

What about Cebes? said Socrates. We must convince Cebes too.

To the best of my belief he is satisfied, replied Simmias. It is true that he is the most obstinate person in the world at resisting an
b argument, but I should think that he needs nothing more to convince him that our souls existed before our birth. As for their existing after we are dead as well, even I don't feel that that has been proved, Socrates. Cebes' objection still holds—the common fear that a man's soul may be disintegrated at the very moment of his death, and that this may be the end of its existence. Supposing that it *is* born and constituted from some source or other, and exists before it enters a human body. After it has entered one, is there any reason why, at the moment of release, it should not come to an end and be destroyed itself?
c   Quite right, Simmias, said Cebes. It seems that we have got the proof of one half of what we wanted—that the soul existed before birth—but now we need also to prove that it will exist after death no less than before birth, if our proof is to be complete.

As a matter of fact, my dear Simmias and Cebes, said Socrates, it is proved already, if you will combine this last argument with the one about which we agreed before, that every living thing comes from the dead. If the soul exists before birth, and if when it proceeds
d toward life and is born it must be born from death or the dead state, surely it must also exist after death, if it must be born again. So the

point which you mention has been proved already. But in spite of this I believe that you and Simmias would like to spin out the discussion still more. You are afraid, as children are, that when the soul emerges from the body the wind may really puff it away and scatter it, especially when a person does not die on a calm day but with a   e gale blowing.

Cebes laughed. Suppose that we are afraid, Socrates, he said, and try to convince us. Or rather don't suppose that it is we that are afraid. Probably even in us there is a little boy who has these childish terrors. Try to persuade him not to be afraid of death as though it were a bogy.

What you should do, said Socrates, is to say a magic spell over him every day until you have charmed his fears away.

But, Socrates, said Simmias, where shall we find a magician who   78 understands these spells now that you . . . are leaving us?

Greece is a large country, Cebes, he replied, which must have good men in it, and there are many foreign races too. You must ransack all of them in your search for this magician, without sparing money or trouble, because you could not spend your money more opportunely on any other object. And you must search also by your own united efforts, because it is probable that you would not easily find anyone better fitted for the task.

We will see to that, said Cebes. But let us return to the point where we left off, if you have no objection.   b

Of course not. Why should I?

Thank you, said Cebes.

We ought, I think, said Socrates, to ask ourselves this. What sort of thing is it that would naturally suffer the fate of being dispersed? For what sort of thing should we fear this fate, and for what should we not? When we have answered this, we should next consider to which class the soul belongs, and then we shall know whether to feel confidence or fear about the fate of our souls.

Quite true.

Would you not expect a composite object or a natural compound   c to be liable to break up where it was put together? And ought not anything which is really incomposite to be the one thing of all others which is not affected in this way?

That seems to be the case, said Cebes.

Is it not extremely probable that what is always constant and invariable is incomposite, and what is inconstant and variable is composite?

That is how it seems to me.

Then let us return to the same examples which we were discussing before. Does that absolute reality which we define in our discus-   d sions remain always constant and invariable, or not? Does absolute equality or beauty or any other independent entity which really exists ever admit change of any kind? Or does each one of these uniform and independent entities remain always constant and invariable, never admitting any alteration in any respect or in any sense?

They must be constant and invariable, Socrates, said Cebes.

Well, what about the concrete instances of beauty—such as men,
e horses, clothes, and so on—or of equality, or any other members of a class corresponding to an absolute entity? Are they constant, or are they, on the contrary, scarcely ever in the same relation in any sense either to themselves or to one another?

With them, Socrates, it is just the opposite; they are never free from variation.

79 And these concrete objects you can touch and see and perceive by your other senses, but those constant entities you cannot possibly apprehend except by thinking; they are invisible to our sight.

That is perfectly true, said Cebes.

So you think that we should assume two classes of things, one visible and the other invisible?

Yes, we should.

The invisible being invariable, and the visible never being the same?

Yes, we should assume that too.
b Well, now, said Socrates, are we not part body, part soul?

Certainly.

Then to which class do we say that the body would have the closer resemblance and relation?

Quite obviously to the visible.

And the soul, is it visible or invisible?

Invisible to men, at any rate, Socrates, he said.

But surely we have been speaking of things visible or invisible to our human nature. Do you think that we had some other nature in view?

No, human nature.

What do we say about the soul, then? Is it visible or invisible?

Not visible.

Invisible, then?

Yes.

So soul is more like the invisible, and body more like the visible?
c That follows inevitably, Socrates.

Did we not say some time ago that when the soul uses the instrumentality of the body for any inquiry, whether through sight or hearing or any other sense—because using the body implies using the senses—it is drawn away by the body into the realm of the variable, and loses its way and becomes confused and dizzy, as though it were fuddled, through contact with things of a similar nature?

Certainly.
d But when it investigates by itself, it passes into the realm of the

pure and everlasting and immortal and changeless, and being of a kindred nature, when it is once independent and free from interference, consorts with it always and strays no longer, but remains, in that realm of the absolute, constant and invariable, through contact with beings of a similar nature. And this condition of the soul we call wisdom.

An excellent description, and perfectly true, Socrates.

Very well, then, in the light of all that we have said, both now and before, to which class do you think that the soul bears the closer e resemblance and relation?

I think, Socrates, said Cebes, that even the dullest person would agree, from this line of reasoning, that the soul is in every possible way more like the invariable than the variable.

And the body?

To the other.

Look at it in this way too. When soul and body are both in the same place, nature teaches the one to serve and be subject, the other 80 to rule and govern. In this relation which do you think resembles the divine and which the mortal part? Don't you think that it is the nature of the divine to rule and direct, and that of the mortal to be subject and serve?

I do.

Then which does the soul resemble?

Obviously, Socrates, soul resembles the divine, and body the mortal.

Now, Cebes, he said, see whether this is our conclusion from all that we have said. The soul is most like that which is divine, im- b mortal, intelligible, uniform, indissoluble, and ever self-consistent and invariable, whereas body is most like that which is human, mortal, multiform, unintelligible, dissoluble, and never self-consistent. Can we adduce any conflicting argument, my dear Cebes, to show that this is not so?

No, we cannot.

Very well, then, in that case is it not natural for body to disintegrate rapidly, but for soul to be quite or very nearly indissoluble?

Certainly. c

Of course you know that when a person dies, although it is natural for the visible and physical part of him, which lies here in the visible world and which we call his corpse, to decay and fall to pieces and be dissipated, none of this happens to it immediately. It remains as it was for quite a long time, even if death takes place when the body is well nourished and in the warm season. Indeed, when the body is dried and embalmed, as in Egypt, it remains almost intact for an incredible time, and even if the rest of the body decays, some parts of it—the bones and sinews and anything else like them—are prac- d tically everlasting. That is so, is it not?

Yes.

But the soul, the invisible part, which goes away to a place that is, like itself, glorious, pure, and invisible—the true Hades or unseen world—into the presence of the good and wise God, where, if God so wills, my soul must shortly go—will it, if its very nature is such as I have described, be dispersed and destroyed at the moment of its re-
e lease from the body, as is the popular view? Far from it, my dear Simmias and Cebes. The truth is much more like this. If at its release the soul is pure and carries with it no contamination of the body, be-cause it has never willingly associated with it in life, but has shunned it and kept itself separate as its regular practice—in other words, if it has pursued philosophy in the right way and really practiced how
81 to face death easily—this is what 'practicing death' means, isn't it?

Most decidedly.

Very well, if this is its condition, then it departs to that place which is, like itself, invisible, divine, immortal, and wise, where, on its arrival, happiness awaits it, and release from uncertainty and folly, from fears and uncontrolled desires, and all other human evils, and where, as they say of the initiates in the Mysteries, it really spends the rest of time with God. Shall we adopt this view, Cebes, or some other?

This one, by all means, said Cebes.

b   But, I suppose, if at the time of its release the soul is tainted and impure, because it has always associated with the body and cared for it and loved it, and has been so beguiled by the body and its passions and pleasures that nothing seems real to it but those physical things which can be touched and seen and eaten and drunk and used for sexual enjoyment, and if it is accustomed to hate and fear and avoid what is invisible and hidden from our eyes, but intelligible and com-prehensible by philosophy—if the soul is in this state, do you think
c that it will escape independent and uncontaminated?

That would be quite impossible, he said.

On the contrary, it will, I imagine, be permeated by the corporeal, which fellowship and intercourse with the body will have ingrained in its very nature through constant association and long practice.

Certainly.

And we must suppose, my dear fellow, that the corporeal is heavy, oppressive, earthly, and visible. So the soul which is tainted by its presence is weighed down and dragged back into the visible world, through fear, as they say, of Hades or the invisible, and hovers
d about tombs and graveyards. The shadowy apparitions which have actually been seen there are the ghosts of those souls which have not got clear away, but still retain some portion of the visible, which is why they can be seen.

That seems likely enough, Socrates.

Yes, it does, Cebes. Of course these are not the souls of the good, but of the wicked, and they are compelled to wander about these places as a punishment for their bad conduct in the past. They continue wandering until at last, through craving for the corporeal, which unceasingly pursues them, they are imprisoned once more in a e body. And as you might expect, they are attached to the same sort of character or nature which they have developed during life.

What sort do you mean, Socrates?

Well, those who have cultivated gluttony or selfishness or drunkenness, instead of taking pains to avoid them, are likely to assume the form of donkeys and other perverse animals. Don't you think so? 82

Yes, that is very likely.

And those who have deliberately preferred a life of irresponsible lawlessness and violence become wolves and hawks and kites, unless we can suggest any other more likely animals.

No, the ones which you mention are exactly right.

So it is easy to imagine into what sort of animals all the other kinds of soul will go, in accordance with their conduct during life.

Yes, certainly.

I suppose that the happiest people, and those who reach the best destination, are the ones who have cultivated the goodness of an ordinary citizen—what is called self-control and integrity—which is acquired by habit and practice, without the help of philosophy and b reason.

How are these the happiest?

Because they will probably pass into some other kind of social and disciplined creature like bees, wasps, and ants, or even back into the human race again, becoming decent citizens.

Very likely.

But no soul which has not practiced philosophy, and is not absolutely pure when it leaves the body, may attain to the divine nature; c that is only for the lover of wisdom. This is the reason, my dear Simmias and Cebes, why true philosophers abstain from all bodily desires and withstand them and do not yield to them. It is not because they are afraid of financial loss or poverty, like the average man who thinks of money first, nor because they shrink from dishonor and a bad reputation, like those who are ambitious for distinction and authority.

No, those would be unworthy motives, Socrates, said Cebes.

They would indeed, he agreed. And so, Cebes, those who care d about their souls and do not subordinate them to the body dissociate themselves firmly from these others and refuse to accompany them on their haphazard journey, and, believing that it is wrong to oppose philosophy with her offer of liberation and purification, they turn and follow her wherever she leads.

What do you mean, Socrates?

I will explain, he said. Every seeker after wisdom knows that up
e to the time when philosophy takes it over his soul is a helpless
prisoner, chained hand and foot in the body, compelled to view
reality not directly but only through its prison bars, and wallowing
in utter ignorance. And philosophy can see that the imprisonment is
83 ingeniously effected by the prisoner's own active desire, which makes
him first accessory to his own confinement. Well, philosophy takes
over the soul in this condition and by gentle persuasion tries to set it
free. She points out that observation by means of the eyes and ears
and all the other senses is entirely deceptive, and she urges the soul to
refrain from using them unless it is necessary to do so, and en-
courages it to collect and concentrate itself by itself, trusting noth-
b ing but its own independent judgment upon objects considered in
themselves, and attributing no truth to anything which it views
indirectly as being subject to variation, because such objects are sensible and visible but what the soul itself sees is intelligible and invisible. Now the soul of the true philosopher feels that it must not reject
this opportunity for release, and so it abstains as far as possible from
pleasures and desires and griefs, because it reflects that the result
of giving way to pleasure or fear or desire is not as might be supposed
the trivial misfortune of becoming ill or wasting money through
c self-indulgence, but the last and worst calamity of all, which the
sufferer does not recognize.

What is that, Socrates? asked Cebes.

When anyone's soul feels a keen pleasure or pain it cannot help
supposing that whatever causes the most violent emotion is the plain-
est and truest reality, which it is not. It is chiefly visible things that
have this effect, isn't it?

Quite so.
d   Is it not on this sort of occasion that soul passes most completely into the bondage of body?

How do you make that out?

Because every pleasure or pain has a sort of rivet with which it
fastens the soul to the body and pins it down and makes it corporeal,
accepting as true whatever the body certifies. The result of agreeing
with the body and finding pleasure in the same things is, I imagine,
that it cannot help becoming like it in character and training, so that
it can never get entirely away to the unseen world, but is always satu-
rated with the body when it sets out, and so soon falls back again into
e another body, where it takes root and grows. Consequently it is ex-
cluded from all fellowship with the pure and uniform and divine.

Yes, that is perfectly true, Socrates, said Cebes.

It is for these reasons, Cebes, that true philosophers exhibit self-
control and courage—not for the reasons which are generally supposed. Or do you think that the popular view is right?
84   No, certainly not.

No, indeed. A philosopher's soul will take the view which I have described. It will not first expect to be set free by philosophy, and then allow pleasure and pain to reduce it once more to bondage, thus taking upon itself an endless task, like Penelope when she undid her own weaving. No, this soul secures immunity from its desires by following reason and abiding always in her company, and by contemplating the true and divine and unconjecturable, and drawing inspiration from it, because such a soul believes that this is the right way to live while life endures, and that after death it reaches a place b which is kindred and similar to its own nature, and there is rid forever of human ills. After such a training, my dear Simmias and Cebes, the soul can have no grounds for fearing that on its separation from the body it will be blown away and scattered by the winds, and so disappear into thin air, and cease to exist altogether.

There was silence for some time after Socrates had said this. He c himself, to judge from his appearance, was still occupied with the argument which he had just been stating, and so were most of us, but Simmias and Cebes went on talking in a low voice.

When Socrates noticed them he said, Why, do you feel that my account is inadequate? Of course it is still open to a number of doubts and objections, if you want to examine it in detail. If it is something else that you two are considering, never mind, but if you feel any difficulty about our discussion, don't hesitate to put forward your own views, and point out any way in which you think that my account could be improved. And by all means make use of my services d too, if you think I can help at all to solve the difficulty.

Very well, Socrates, said Simmias, I will be quite open with you. We have both been feeling difficulties for some time, and each of us has been urging the other to ask questions. We are anxious to have your answers, but we did not like to bother you, for fear of annoying you in your present misfortune.

When Socrates heard this he laughed gently and said, I am surprised at you, Simmias. I shall certainly find it difficult to convince the outside world that I do not regard my present lot as a misfortune if I cannot even convince you, and you are afraid that I am more e irritable now than I used to be. Evidently you think that I have less insight into the future than a swan; because when these birds feel that the time has come for them to die, they sing more loudly and sweetly than they have sung in all their lives before, for joy that they are going away into the presence of the god whose servants they are. It is 85 quite wrong for human beings to make out that the swans sing their last song as an expression of grief at their approaching end. People who say this are misled by their own fear of death, and fail to reflect that no bird sings when it is hungry or cold or distressed in any other way—not even the nightingale or swallow or hoopoe, whose song is supposed to be a lament. In my opinion neither they nor the swans

sing because they are sad. I believe that the swans, belonging as they
b do to Apollo, have prophetic powers and sing because they know the
good things that await them in the unseen world, and they are happier on that day than they have ever been before. Now I consider that
I am in the same service as the swans, and dedicated to the same god,
and that I am no worse endowed with prophetic powers by my master
than they are, and no more disconsolate at leaving this life. So far as
that fear of yours is concerned, you may say and ask whatever you
like, so long as the Athenian officers of justice permit.

Thank you, said Simmias. I will tell you my difficulty first and
c then Cebes shall tell you where he finds your theory unacceptable. I
think, just as you do, Socrates, that although it is very difficult if not
impossible in this life to achieve certainty about these questions, at
the same time it is utterly feeble not to use every effort in testing the
available theories, or to leave off before we have considered them
in every way, and come to the end of our resources. It is our duty to do
one of two things, either to ascertain the facts, whether by seeking
instruction or by personal discovery, or, if this is impossible, to select
the best and most dependable theory which human intelligence can
d supply, and use it as a raft to ride the seas of life—that is, assuming
that we cannot make our journey with greater confidence and security by the surer means of a divine revelation. And so now, after what
you have said, I shall not let any diffidence prevent me from asking
my question, and so make me blame myself afterward for not having
spoken my mind now. The fact is, Socrates, that on thinking it over,
and discussing it with Cebes here, I feel that your theory has serious flaws in it.

e Your feeling is very likely right, my dear boy, said Socrates, but
tell me where you think the flaws are.

What I mean is this, said Simmias. You might say the same
thing about tuning the strings of a musical instrument, that the attunement is something invisible and incorporeal and splendid and
divine, and located in the tuned instrument, while the instrument
86 itself and its strings are material and corporeal and composite and
earthly and closely related to what is mortal. Now suppose that the
instrument is broken, or its strings cut or snapped. According to your
theory the attunement must still exist—it cannot have been destroyed,
because it would be inconceivable that when the strings are broken
the instrument and the strings themselves, which have a mortal
nature, should still exist, and the attunement, which shares the nature
and characteristics of the divine and immortal, should exist no
b longer, having predeceased its mortal counterpart. You would say
that the attunement must still exist somewhere just as it was, and
that the wood and strings will rot away before anything happens to it.
I say this, Socrates, because, as I think you yourself are aware, we
Pythagoreans have a theory of the soul which is roughly like this.

The body is held together at a certain tension between the extremes of hot and cold, and dry and wet, and so on, and our soul is a temperament or adjustment of these same extremes, when they are combined in just the right proportion. Well, if the soul is really an adjustment, c obviously as soon as the tension of our body is lowered or increased beyond the proper point, the soul must be destroyed, divine though it is—just like any other adjustment, either in music or in any product of the arts and crafts, although in each case the physical remains last considerably longer until they are burned up or rot away. Find us an answer to this argument, if someone insists that the soul, being a d temperament of physical constituents, is the first thing to be destroyed by what we call death.

Socrates opened his eyes very wide—a favorite trick of his—and smiled. Really, he said, Simmias' criticism is quite justified, so if any of you are readier-witted than I am, you had better answer him. It seems to me that he is not handling the argument at all badly. However, before we have the answer, I think we should hear what criticisms Cebes has to make in his turn, so that we may have time e to decide what we shall say. When we have heard him, we must either agree with them if they seem to be at all on the right note, or if not, we must then proceed to champion our theory.

Come on, Cebes, he said, tell us what has been troubling you.

Very well, said Cebes. It seems to me that the argument is just where it was. I mean that it is open to the same criticism that we made before. The proof that our soul existed before it took on this 87 present shape is perfectly satisfying—I might even say convincing. I am not changing my position about that. But as for its still existing somewhere after we are dead, I think that the proof fails in this way. Mind you, I don't agree with Simmias' objection that soul is not stronger and more durable than body; it seems to me to be far superior in every way like that. Then why, your theory might inquire, are you still skeptical, when you can see that after a man dies even the weaker part of him continues to exist? Don't you think the more durable part of him must logically survive as long?

Well, here is my answer. I want you to consider whether there is b anything in what I say—because like Simmias I must have recourse to an illustration. Suppose that an elderly tailor has just died. Your theory would be just like saying that the man is not dead, but still exists somewhere safe and sound, and offering as proof the fact that the coat which he had made for himself and was wearing has not perished but is still intact. If anyone was skeptical, I suppose you would ask him which is likely to last longer, a man or a coat which is c being regularly used and worn, and when he replied that the former was far more likely, you would imagine that you had proved conclusively that the man is safe and sound, since the less-enduring object has not perished. But surely this is not so, Simmias—because I

want your opinion too. Anyone would dismiss such a view as absurd. The tailor makes and wears out any number of coats, but although he
d outlives all the others, presumably he perishes before the last one, and this does not mean that a man is inferior to a coat, or has a weaker hold upon life. I believe that this analogy might apply to the relation of soul to body, and I think that it would be reasonable to say of them in the same way that soul is a long-lived thing, whereas body is relatively feeble and short-lived. But while we may admit that each soul wears out a number of bodies, especially if it lives a great many years—because although the body is continually changing and disintegrating all through life, the soul never stops replacing what is worn
e away—still we must suppose that when the soul dies it is still in possession of its latest covering, and perishes before it in this case only, although when the soul has perished the body at last reveals its natural frailty and quickly rots away. If you accept this view there is no justification yet for any confidence that after death our souls still exist somewhere.

88   Suppose that one conceded to the exponent of immortality even more than you claim, granting not only that our souls existed before our birth, but also that some of them may continue to exist or come into existence after death, and be born and die again several times— soul having such natural vitality that it persists through successive incarnations—unless in granting this he made the further concession that the soul suffers no ill effects in its various rebirths, and so does not, at one of its 'deaths,' perish altogether. If he had to admit that nobody knows which of these 'deaths' or separations from the body
b may prove fatal to the soul, because such insight is impossible for any of us—on these terms, Socrates, no one but a fool is entitled to face death with confidence, unless he can prove that the soul is absolutely immortal and indestructible. Otherwise everyone must always feel apprehension at the approach of death, for fear that in this particular separation from the body his soul may be finally and utterly destroyed.

c   Well, when we had heard them state their objections, we all felt very much depressed, as we told one another later. We had been quite convinced by the earlier part of the discussion, and now we felt that they had upset our convictions and destroyed our confidence not only in what had been said already, but also in anything that was to follow later. Perhaps we were incompetent to judge, or the facts themselves might prove to be unreliable.

ECHECRATES : You certainly have my full sympathy, Phaedo. After hearing your account I find myself faced with the same mis-
d giving. How can we believe in anything after this? Socrates' argument was absolutely convincing, and now it is completely discredited. That theory that our soul is a sort of attunement has always had an extraordinary attraction for me, and when I heard it stated it reminded

me that I myself had formed the same opinion. What I really need now is another proof, right from the beginning, to convince me that when a man dies his soul does not die with him. Tell me, how did Socrates pick up the trail again? And did he show any sign of being e upset, like the rest of you, or did he quietly come to the rescue of the argument? And did he rescue it effectively or not? Tell us every detail as accurately as you can.

PHAEDO: I can assure you, Echecrates, that Socrates often astonished me, but I never admired him more than on this particu- 89 lar occasion. That he should have been ready with an answer was, I suppose, nothing unusual, but what impressed me was, first, the pleasant, kindly, appreciative way in which he received the two boys' objections, then his quick recognition of how the turn of the discussion had affected us, and lastly the skill with which he healed our wounds, rallied our scattered forces, and encouraged us to join him in pursuing the inquiry.

ECHECRATES: How did he do that?

PHAEDO: I will tell you. I happened to be sitting to the right of his bed, on a footstool, and he was much higher than I was. So he b laid his hand on my head and gathered up the curls on my neck—he never missed a chance of teasing me about my curls—and said, To-morrow, I suppose, Phaedo, you will cut off this beautiful hair.

I expect so, Socrates, I said.

Not if you take my advice.

Why not? I asked.

Because I shall cut off mine today, and you ought to do the same, said Socrates, that is, if we let our argument die and fail to bring it to life again. What is more, if I were you, and let the truth escape me, I should make a vow like the Argives' never to let my hair grow c again until I had defeated the argument of Simmias and Cebes in a return battle.

But, I objected, not even Heracles can take on two at once.

You had better call upon me to be your Iolaus, he said, while the daylight lasts.

Very well, I said, but I am Iolaus appealing to Heracles, not Heracles to Iolaus.

The effect will be just the same, he said. But first there is one danger that we must guard against.

What sort of danger? I asked.

Of becoming misologic, he said, in the sense that people become d misanthropic. No greater misfortune could happen to anyone than that of developing a dislike for argument. Misology and misanthropy arise in just the same way. Misanthropy is induced by believing in somebody quite uncritically. You assume that a person is absolutely truthful and sincere and reliable, and a little later you find that he is shoddy and unreliable. Then the same thing happens again. After

repeated disappointments at the hands of the very people who might
e be supposed to be your nearest and most intimate friends, constant
irritation ends by making you dislike everybody and suppose that
there is no sincerity to be found anywhere. Have you never noticed
this happening?

Indeed, I have.

Don't you feel that it is reprehensible? Isn't it obvious that such
a person is trying to form human relationships without any critical
understanding of human nature? Otherwise he would surely recognize the truth—that there are not many very good or very bad people,
90 but the great majority are something between the two.

How do you make that out? I asked.

On the analogy of very large or small objects, he said. Can you
think of anything more unusual than coming across a very large or
small man, or dog, or any other creature? Or one which is very swift
or slow, ugly or beautiful, white or black? Have you never realized
that extreme instances are few and rare, while intermediate ones are
many and plentiful?

Certainly.

b   So you think that if there were a competition in wickedness,
very few would distinguish themselves even there?

Probably.

Yes, it is probable, said Socrates. However, you have led me
into a digression. The resemblance between arguments and human
beings lies not in what I said just now, but in what I said before, that
when one believes that an argument is true without reference to the
art of logic, and then a little later decides rightly or wrongly that it is
false, and the same thing happens again and again—you know how
c it is, especially with those who spend their time in arguing both sides
—they end by believing that they are wiser than anyone else, because
they alone have discovered that there is nothing stable or dependable
either in facts or in arguments, and that everything fluctuates just like
the water in a tidal channel, and never stays at any point for any
time.

That is perfectly true, I said.

Well, then, Phaedo, he said, supposing that there is an argument
which is true and valid and capable of being discovered, if anyone
d nevertheless, through his experience of these arguments which seem
to the same people to be sometimes true and sometimes false, attached no responsibility to himself and his lack of technical ability,
but was finally content, in exasperation, to shift the blame from himself to the arguments, and spend the rest of his life loathing and
decrying them, and so missed the chance of knowing the truth about
reality—would it not be a deplorable thing?

It would indeed, I said.

Very well, he said, that is the first thing that we must guard

against. We must not let it enter our minds that there may be no e
validity in argument. On the contrary we should recognize that we
ourselves are still intellectual invalids, but that we must brace ourselves and do our best to become healthy—you and the others partly
with a view to the rest of your lives, but I directly in view of my
death, because at the moment I am in danger of regarding it not phil- 91
osophically but self-assertively. You know how, in an argument, people who have no real education care nothing for the facts of the case,
and are only anxious to get their point of view accepted by the audience? Well, I feel that at this present moment I am as bad as they are,
only with this difference, that my anxiety will be not to convince my
audience, except incidentally, but to produce the strongest possible
conviction in myself. This is how I weigh the position, my dear fellow—see how selfish I am! If my theory is really true, it is right to be- b
lieve it, while, even if death is extinction, at any rate during this time
before my death I shall be less likely to distress my companions by
giving way to self-pity, and this folly of mine will not live on with me
—which would be a calamity—but will shortly come to an end.

That, my dear Simmias and Cebes, is the spirit in which I am
prepared to approach the discussion. As for you, if you will take my
advice, you will think very little of Socrates, and much more of the
truth. If you think that anything I say is true, you must agree with c
me; if not, oppose it with every argument that you have. You must
not allow me, in my enthusiasm, to deceive both myself and you, and
leave my sting behind when I fly away.

Well, we must go ahead, he continued. First remind me of what
you said, if you find my memory inaccurate. Simmias, I believe, is
troubled with doubts. He is afraid that, even if the soul is more divine
and a higher thing than the body, it may nevertheless be destroyed
first, as being a kind of attunement. Cebes on the other hand appeared d
to agree with me that soul is more enduring than body, but to maintain that no one can be sure that, after repeatedly wearing out a great
many bodies, it does not at last perish itself, leaving the last body behind; and he thinks that death may be precisely this, the destruction
of the soul, because the body never stops perishing all the time. Am I
right, Simmias and Cebes, in thinking that these are the objections
which we have to investigate?

They agreed that this was so. e

Well, then, he said, do you reject all our previous arguments,
or only some of them?

Only some of them, they said.

What is your opinion of the reasoning by which we asserted that
learning is recollection, and that, if this is so, our souls must have
existed somewhere else before they were confined in the body? 92

Speaking for myself, said Cebes, I found it remarkably convincing at the time, and I stick to it still as I do to no other theory.

Yes, indeed, said Simmias, it is just the same with me. I should be very much surprised if I ever changed my opinion about that.

But you will have to change it, my Theban friend, said Socrates, if the conception stands that an attunement is a composite thing, and that the soul is an attunement composed of our physical elements at a given tension. I imagine that you would not accept even from

b yourself the assertion that a composite attunement existed before the elements of which it was to be composed. Or would you?

Not for a moment, Socrates.

Don't you see that that is just what it amounts to when you say that the soul exists before it enters the human form or body, and also that it is composed of elements which do not yet exist? Surely an attunement is not at all like the object of your comparison. The in-

c strument and the strings and their untuned notes come first. The attunement is the last of all to be constituted and the first to be destroyed. How will this account harmonize with the other?

Not at all, said Simmias.

And yet, said Socrates, if any account ought to be harmonious, it should be an account of attunement.

Yes, it should, said Simmias.

Well, said Socrates, this one does not harmonize with your view. Make up your mind which theory you prefer—that learning is recollection, or that soul is an attunement.

The former, without any hesitation, Socrates, he said. The other appealed to me, without any proof to support it, as being based on

d plausible analogy, which is why most people find it attractive. But I realize that theories which rest their proof upon plausibility are impostors, and unless you are on your guard, they deceive you properly, both in geometry and everywhere else. On the other hand, the theory of recollection and learning derives from a hypothesis which is worthy of acceptance. The theory that our soul exists even before it enters the body surely stands or falls with the soul's possession of the ultimate standard of reality—a view which I have, to the best of my

e belief, fully and rightly accepted. It seems therefore that I must not accept, either from myself or from anyone else, the assertion that soul is an attunement.

There is this way of looking at it too, Simmias, said Socrates. Do you think that an attunement, or any other composite thing, should

93 be in a condition different from that of its component elements?

No, I do not.

And it should not act, or be acted upon, I presume, differently from them?

He agreed.

So an attunement should not control its elements, but should follow their lead?

He assented.

There is no question of its conflicting with them, either in movement or in sound or in any other way.

None at all.

Very well, then, is it not the nature of every attunement to be an attunement in so far as it is tuned?

I don't understand.

Surely, said Socrates, if it is tuned more, that is, in a greater degree—supposing this to be possible—it must be more of an attune- b ment, and if it is tuned less, that is, in a lesser degree, it must be less of an attunement.

Quite so.

And is this the case with the soul—that one soul is, even minutely, more or less of a soul than another?

Not in the least.

Now please give me your closest attention, said Socrates. Do we say that one kind of soul possesses intelligence and goodness, and is good, and that another possesses stupidity and wickedness, and is evil? And is this true? c

Yes, it is true.

Then how will a person who holds that the soul is an attunement account for the presence in it of goodness and badness? Will he describe them as yet another attunement or lack of it? Will he say that the good soul is in tune, and not only is an attunement itself, but contains another, whereas the bad soul is out of tune and does not contain another attunement?

I really could not say, replied Simmias, but obviously anyone who held that view would have to say something of the sort.

But we have already agreed, said Socrates, that no soul can be d more or less of a soul than another, and this is the same as agreeing that no attunement can be more of an attunement and in a greater degree, or less of an attunement and in a lesser degree, than another. Is that not so?

Certainly.

And that what is neither more nor less of an attunement is neither more nor less in tune. Is that so?

Yes.

Does that which is neither more nor less in tune contain a greater or smaller proportion of attunement, or an equal one? e

An equal one.

Then since no soul is any more or less than just a soul, it is neither more nor less in tune.

That is so.

Under this condition it cannot contain a greater proportion of discord or attunement.

Certainly not.

And again under this condition can one soul contain a greater proportion of badness or goodness than another, assuming that badness is discord and goodness attunement?

No, it cannot.

94   Or rather, I suppose, Simmias, by strict reasoning no soul will contain any share of badness, if it is an attunement, because surely since attunement is absolutely attunement and nothing else, it can never contain any share of discord.

No, indeed.

Nor can the soul, since it is absolutely soul, contain a share of badness.

Not in the light of what we have said.

So on this theory every soul of every living creature will be equally good—assuming that it is the nature of all souls to be equally souls and nothing else.

I think that follows, Socrates.

Do you also think that this view is right? Would the argument
b ever have come to this if our hypothesis, that the soul is an attunement, had been correct?

Not the least chance of it.

Well, said Socrates, do you hold that it is any other part of a man than the soul that governs him, especially if it is a wise one?

No, I do not.

Does it yield to the feelings of the body, or oppose them? I mean, for instance, that when a person is feverish and thirsty it impels him the other way, not to drink, and when he is hungry, not to eat, and
c there are thousands of other ways in which we see the soul opposing the physical instincts. Is that not so?

Certainly.

Did we not also agree a little while ago that if it is an attunement it can never sound a note that conflicts with the tension or relaxation or vibration or any other condition of its constituents, but must always follow them and never direct them?

Yes, we did, of course.

Well, surely we can see now that the soul works in just the opposite way. It directs all the elements of which it is said to consist, opposing them in almost everything all through life, and exercising
d every form of control—sometimes by severe and unpleasant methods like those of physical training and medicine, and sometimes by milder ones, sometimes scolding, sometimes encouraging—and conversing with the desires and passions and fears as though it were quite separate and distinct from them. It is just like Homer's description in the *Odyssey* where he says that Odysseus

> Then beat his breast, and thus reproved his heart,
e > Endure, my heart; still worse hast thou endured.[1]

[1] *Odyssey* 20.17 sq.

Do you suppose that when he wrote that he thought that the soul was an attunement, liable to be swayed by physical feelings? Surely he regarded it as capable of swaying and controlling them, as something much too divine to rank as an attunement.

That is certainly how it seems to me, Socrates.

Good. In that case there is no justification for our saying that soul is a kind of attunement. We should neither agree with Homer nor 95 be consistent ourselves.

That is so.

Well now, said Socrates, we seem to have placated the Theban lady Harmonia with moderate success. But what about Cadmus, Cebes? How shall we placate him, and what argument shall we use?

I think that you will find a way, said Cebes. This argument which you brought forward against the attunement theory far surpassed all my expectations. When Simmias was explaining his difficulties I wondered very much whether anyone would be able to do b anything with his argument; so I was quite astonished that it could not stand up against your very first attack. I should not be surprised if Cadmus' argument met the same fate.

My dear fellow, said Socrates, don't boast, or some misfortune will upset the forthcoming argument. However, we will leave that to God; it is our task to come to close quarters in the Homeric manner and test the validity of your contention.

What you require, in a nutshell, is this. You consider that unless the confidence of a philosopher who at the point of dying believes c that after death he will be better off for having lived and ended his life in philosophy than in any other way of living is to be a blind and foolish confidence, the soul must be proved to be indestructible and immortal. To show that it has great vitality and a godlike nature, and even that it existed before we were born—all this, you say, may very well indicate not that the soul is immortal, but merely that it is long-lived, and pre-existed somewhere for a prodigious period of time, enjoying a great measure of knowledge and activity. But all this did not make it any the more immortal. Indeed its very entrance into the d human body was, like a disease, the beginning of its destruction; it lives this life in increasing weariness, and finally perishes in what we call death. You also say that, to our individual fears, it makes no difference whether it enters the body once or often. Anyone who does not know and cannot prove that the soul is immortal must be afraid, unless he is a fool.

That, I believe, is the substance of your objection, Cebes. I am deliberately reviewing it more than once, in order that nothing may es- e cape us, and that you may add to it or subtract from it anything that you wish.

Cebes said, But at the present moment there is no need for me to add or subtract anything; that is precisely my point of view.

After spending some time in reflection Socrates said, What you require is no light undertaking, Cebes. It involves a full treatment of the causes of generation and destruction. If you like, I will describe
96 my own experiences in this connection, and then, if you find anything helpful in my account, you can use it to reassure yourself about your own objections.

Yes, indeed, said Cebes, I should like that very much.

Then listen, and I will tell you. When I was young, Cebes, I had an extraordinary passion for that branch of learning which is called natural science. I thought it would be marvelous to know the causes for which each thing comes and ceases and continues to be. I was
b constantly veering to and fro, puzzling primarily over this sort of question. Is it when heat and cold produce fermentation, as some have said, that living creatures are bred? Is it with the blood that we think, or with the air or the fire that is in us? Or is it none of these, but the brain that supplies our senses of hearing and sight and smell, and from these that memory and opinion arise, and from memory and opinion, when established, that knowledge comes? Then again I
c would consider how these faculties are lost, and study celestial and terrestrial phenomena, until at last I came to the conclusion that I was uniquely unfitted for this form of inquiry. I will give you a sufficient indication of what I mean. I had understood some things plainly before, in my own and other people's estimation, but now I was so befogged by these speculations that I unlearned even what I had thought I knew, especially about the cause of growth in human beings. Previously I had thought that it was quite obviously due to eating and
d drinking—that when, from the food which we consume, flesh is added to flesh and bone to bone, and when in the same way the other parts of the body are augmented by their appropriate particles, the bulk which was small is now large, and in this way the small man becomes a big one. That is what I used to believe—reasonably, don't you think?

Yes, I do, said Cebes.

Consider a little further. I had been content to think, when I saw a tall man standing beside a short one, that he was taller by a head, and similarly in the case of horses. And it seemed to me even more
e obvious that ten is more than eight because it contains two more, and that two feet is bigger than one because it exceeds it by half its own length.

And what do you believe about them now? asked Cebes.

Why, upon my word, that I am very far from supposing that I know the explanation of any of these things. I cannot even convince myself that when you add one to one either the first or the second
97 one becomes two, or they both become two by the addition of the one to the other. I find it hard to believe that, although when they were separate each of them was one and they were not two, now that they

have come together the cause of their becoming two is simply the union caused by their juxtaposition. Nor can I believe now, when you divide one, that this time the cause of its becoming two is the division, because this cause of its becoming two is the opposite of the b former one; then it was because they were brought close together and added one to the other, but now it is because they are taken apart and separated one from the other. Nor can I now persuade myself that I understand how it is that things become one, nor, in short, why anything else comes or ceases or continues to be, according to this method of inquiry. So I reject it altogether, and muddle out a haphazard method of my own.

However, I once heard someone reading from a book, as he said, by Anaxagoras, and asserting that it is mind that produces order and c is the cause of everything. This explanation pleased me. Somehow it seemed right that mind should be the cause of everything, and I reflected that if this is so, mind in producing order sets everything in order and arranges each individual thing in the way that is best for it. Therefore if anyone wished to discover the reason why any given thing came or ceased or continued to be, he must find out how it was best for that thing to be, or to act or be acted upon in any other way. On d this view there was only one thing for a man to consider, with regard both to himself and to anything else, namely the best and highest good, although this would necessarily imply knowing what is less good, since both were covered by the same knowledge.

These reflections made me suppose, to my delight, that in Anaxagoras I had found an authority on causation who was after my own heart. I assumed that he would begin by informing us whether the earth is flat or round, and would then proceed to explain in detail e the reason and logical necessity for this by stating how and why it was better that it should be so. I thought that if he asserted that the earth was in the center, he would explain in detail that it was better for it to be there; and if he made this clear, I was prepared to give up 98 hankering after any other kind of cause. I was prepared also in the same way to receive instruction about the sun and moon and the other heavenly bodies, about their relative velocities and their orbits and all the other phenomena connected with them—in what way it is better for each one of them to act or be acted upon as it is. It never entered my head that a man who asserted that the ordering of things is due to mind would offer any other explanation for them than that it is best for them to be as they are. I thought that by assigning a cause to each phenomenon separately and to the universe as a whole b he would make perfectly clear what is best for each and what is the universal good. I would not have parted with my hopes for a great sum of money. I lost no time in procuring the books, and began to read them as quickly as I possibly could, so that I might know as soon as possible about the best and the less good.

It was a wonderful hope, my friend, but it was quickly dashed. As I read on I discovered that the fellow made no use of mind and assigned to it no causality for the order of the world, but adduced
c causes like air and æther and water and many other absurdities. It seemed to me that he was just about as inconsistent as if someone were to say, The cause of everything that Socrates does is mind— and then, in trying to account for my several actions, said first that the reason why I am lying here now is that my body is composed of bones and sinews, and that the bones are rigid and separated at the
d joints, but the sinews are capable of contraction and relaxation, and form an envelope for the bones with the help of the flesh and skin, the latter holding all together, and since the bones move freely in their joints the sinews by relaxing and contracting enable me some- how to bend my limbs, and that is the cause of my sitting here in a bent position. Or again, if he tried to account in the same way for my conversing with you, adducing causes such as sound and air and hear- ing and a thousand others, and never troubled to mention the real
e reasons, which are that since Athens has thought it better to condemn me, therefore I for my part have thought it better to sit here, and more right to stay and submit to whatever penalty she orders. Because,
99 by dog, I fancy that these sinews and bones would have been in the neighborhood of Megara or Boeotia long ago—impelled by a convic- tion of what is best!—if I did not think that it was more right and honorable to submit to whatever penalty my country orders rather than take to my heels and run away. But to call things like that causes is too absurd. If it were said that without such bones and sinews and all the rest of them I should not be able to do what I think is right, it would be true. But to say that it is because of them that I
b do what I am doing, and not through choice of what is best—al- though my actions are controlled by mind—would be a very lax and inaccurate form of expression. Fancy being unable to distinguish between the cause of a thing and the condition without which it could not be a cause! It is this latter, as it seems to me, that most peo- ple, groping in the dark, call a cause—attaching to it a name to which it has no right. That is why one person surrounds the earth with a vortex, and so keeps it in place by means of the heavens, and another props it up on a pedestal of air, as though it were a wide platter. As for a power which keeps things disposed at any given moment in
c the best possible way, they neither look for it nor believe that it has any supernatural force. They imagine that they will someday find a more mighty and immortal and all-sustaining Atlas, and they do not think that anything is really bound and held together by goodness or moral obligation. For my part, I should be delighted to learn about the workings of such a cause from anyone, but since I have been de- nied knowledge of it, and have been unable either to discover it my- self or to learn about it from another, I have worked out my own

makeshift approach to the problem of causation. Would you like me
to give you a demonstration of it, Cebes?   d

I should like it very much indeed.

Well, after this, said Socrates, when I was worn out with my
physical investigations, it occurred to me that I must guard against
the same sort of risk which people run when they watch and study
an eclipse of the sun; they really do sometimes injure their eyes, unless they study its reflection in water or some other medium. I con-
ceived of something like this happening to myself, and I was afraid
that by observing objects with my eyes and trying to comprehend them
with each of my other senses I might blind my soul altogether. So I   e
decided that I must have recourse to theories, and use them in trying
to discover the truth about things. Perhaps my illustration is not
quite apt, because I do not at all admit that an inquiry by means of 100
theory employs 'images' any more than one which confines itself to
facts. But however that may be, I started off in this way, and in every
case I first lay down the theory which I judge to be soundest, and
then whatever seems to agree with it—with regard either to causes or
to anything else—I assume to be true, and whatever does not I assume
not to be true. But I should like to express my meaning more clearly,
because at present I don't think that you understand.

No, indeed I don't, said Cebes, not a bit.

Well, said Socrates, what I mean is this, and there is nothing new b
about it. I have always said it; in fact I have never stopped saying it,
especially in the earlier part of this discussion. As I am going to try
to explain to you the theory of causation which I have worked out
myself, I propose to make a fresh start from those principles of mine
which you know so well—that is, I am assuming the existence of absolute beauty and goodness and magnitude and all the rest of
them. If you grant my assumption and admit that they exist, I hope
with their help to explain causation to you, and to find a proof that
soul is immortal.

Certainly I grant it, said Cebes. You need lose no time in draw- c
ing your conclusion.

Then consider the next step, and see whether you share my opinion. It seems to me that whatever else is beautiful apart from absolute
beauty is beautiful because it partakes of that absolute beauty, and for
no other reason. Do you accept this kind of causality?

Yes, I do.

Well, now, that is as far as my mind goes; I cannot understand
these other ingenious theories of causation. If someone tells me that
the reason why a given object is beautiful is that it has a gorgeous d
color or shape or any other such attribute, I disregard all these other
explanations—I find them all confusing—and I cling simply and
straightforwardly and no doubt foolishly to the explanation that the
one thing that makes that object beautiful is the presence in it or

association with it, in whatever way the relation comes about, of absolute beauty. I do not go so far as to insist upon the precise details —only upon the fact that it is by beauty that beautiful things are beautiful. This, I feel, is the safest answer for me or for anyone else to give, and I believe that while I hold fast to this I cannot fall; it is safe

e for me or for anyone else to answer that it is by beauty that beautiful things are beautiful. Don't you agree?

Yes, I do.

Then is it also by largeness that large things are large and larger things larger, and by smallness that smaller things are smaller?

Yes.

So you too, like myself, would refuse to accept the statement that one man is taller than another 'by a head,' and that the shorter man is shorter by the same. You would protest that the only view

101 which you yourself can hold is that whatever is taller than something else is so simply by tallness—that is, because of tallness— and that what is shorter is so simply by shortness, that is, because of shortness. You would be afraid, I suppose, that if you said that one man is taller than another by a head, you would be faced by a logical objection—first that the taller should be taller and the shorter shorter by the same thing, and secondly that the taller person should be taller by a head, which is a short thing, and that it is unnatural that

b a man should be made tall by something short. Isn't that so?

Cebes laughed and said, Yes, it is.

Then you would be afraid to say that ten is more than eight 'by two,' or that two is the cause of its excess over eight, instead of saying that it is more than eight by, or because of, being a larger number, and you would be afraid to say that a length of two feet is greater than one foot by a half, instead of saying that it is greater by its larger size—because there is the same danger here too?

Quite so.

Suppose next that we add one to one. You would surely avoid say-

c ing that the cause of our getting two is the addition, or in the case of a divided unit, the division. You would loudly proclaim that you know of no other way in which any given object can come into being except by participation in the reality peculiar to its appropriate universal, and that in the cases which I have mentioned you recognize no other cause for the coming into being of two than participation in duality, and that whatever is to become two must participate in this, and whatever is to become one must participate in unity. You would dismiss these divisions and additions and other such niceties, leaving them for persons wiser than yourself to use in their explanations,

d while you, being nervous of your own shadow, as the saying is, and of your inexperience, would hold fast to the security of your hypothesis and make your answers accordingly. If anyone should fasten upon the hypothesis itself, you would disregard him and refuse to answer until you could consider whether its consequences were mutually consistent or not. And when you had to substantiate the hypothesis itself, you would proceed in the same way, assuming whatever more ultimate hypothesis commended itself most to you, until you reached one which was satisfactory. You would not mix the two things together e by discussing both the principle and its consequences, like one of these destructive critics—that is, if you wanted to discover any part of the truth. They presumably have no concern or care whatever for such an object, because their cleverness enables them to muddle everything up without disturbing their own self-complacence, but you, I imagine, if you are a philosopher, will follow the course which I describe.   102

You are perfectly right, said Simmias and Cebes together.

ECHECRATES : I can assure you, Phaedo, I am not surprised. It seems to me that Socrates made his meaning extraordinarily clear to even a limited intelligence.

PHAEDO : That was certainly the feeling of all of us who were present, Echecrates.

ECHECRATES : No doubt, because it is just the same with us who were not present and are hearing it now for the first time. But how did the discussion go on?

PHAEDO : I think that when Socrates had got this accepted, and it was agreed that the various forms exist, and that the reason why b other things are called after the forms is that they participate in the forms, he next went on to ask, If you hold this view, I suppose that when you say that Simmias is taller than Socrates but shorter than Phaedo, you mean that at that moment there are in Simmias both tallness and shortness?

Yes, I do.

But do you agree that the statement 'Simmias is bigger than Socrates' is not true in the form in which it is expressed? Surely the real reason why Simmias is bigger is not because he is Simmias but because of the height which he incidentally possesses, and conversely c the reason why he is bigger than Socrates is not because Socrates is Socrates, but because Socrates has the attribute of shortness in comparison with Simmias' height.

True.

And again Simmias' being smaller than Phaedo is due not to the fact that Phaedo is Phaedo, but to the fact that Phaedo has the attribute of tallness in comparison with Simmias' shortness.

Quite so.

So that is how Simmias comes to be described as both short and tall, because he is intermediate between the two of them, and allows his shortness to be surpassed by the tallness of the one while he as- d serts his superior tallness over the shortness of the other.

He added with a smile, I seem to be developing an artificial style, but the facts are surely as I say.

Simmias agreed.

I am saying all this because I want you to share my point of view. It seems to me not only that the form of tallness itself absolutely declines to be short as well as tall, but also that the tallness which is in us never admits smallness and declines to be surpassed. It does one of two things. Either it gives way and withdraws as its opposite shortness approaches, or it has already ceased to exist by the time that the other arrives. It cannot stand its ground and receive the quality of shortness in the same way as I myself have done. If it did, it would become different from what it was before, whereas I have not lost my identity by acquiring the quality of shortness—I am the same man, only short —but my tallness could not endure to be short instead of tall. In the same way the shortness that is in us declines ever to become or be tall, nor will any other quality, while still remaining what it was, at the same time become or be the opposite quality; in such a situation it either withdraws or ceases to exist.

I agree with you entirely, said Cebes.

At this point one of the company—I can't remember distinctly who it was—said, Look here! Didn't we agree, earlier in the discussion, on the exact opposite of what you are saying now—that the bigger comes from the smaller and the smaller from the bigger, and that it is precisely from their opposites that opposites come? Now the view seems to be that this is impossible.

Socrates had listened with his head turned toward the speaker. It was brave of you to refresh my memory, he said, but you don't realize the difference between what we are saying now and what we said then. Then we were saying that opposite *things* come from opposite *things;* now we are saying that the opposite *itself* can never become opposite to *itself*—neither the opposite which is in us nor that which is in the real world. Then, my friend, we were speaking about objects which possess opposite qualities, and calling them by the names of the latter, but now we are speaking about the qualities themselves, from whose presence in them the objects which are called after them derive their names. We maintain that the opposites themselves would absolutely refuse to tolerate coming into being from one another.

As he spoke he looked at Cebes. I suppose that nothing in what he said worried you too, Cebes?

No, not this time, said Cebes, though I don't deny that a good many other things do.

So we are agreed upon this as a general principle, that an opposite can never be opposite to itself.

Absolutely.

Then consider this point too, and see whether you agree about it too. Do you admit that there are such things as heat and cold?

Yes, I do.

Do you think they are the same as snow and fire?

Certainly not.

Heat is quite distinct from fire, and cold from snow?

Yes.

But I suppose you agree, in the light of what we said before, that snow, being what it is, can never admit heat and still remain snow, just as it was before, only with the addition of heat. It must either withdraw at the approach of heat, or cease to exist.

Quite so.

Again, fire must either retire or cease to exist at the approach of cold. It will never have the courage to admit cold and still remain fire, just as it was, only with the addition of cold.

That is true. e

So we find, in certain cases like these, that the name of the form is eternally applicable not only to the form itself, but also to something else, which is not the form but invariably possesses its distinguishing characteristic. But perhaps another example will make my meaning clearer. Oddness must always be entitled to this name by which I am now calling it, isn't that so?

Certainly.

This is the question. Is it unique in this respect, or is there something else, not identical with oddness, to which we are bound always 104 to apply not only its own name but that of odd as well, because by its very nature it never loses its oddness? What I mean is illustrated by the case of the number three; there are plenty of other examples, but take the case of three. Don't you think that it must always be described not only by its own name but by that of odd, although odd and three are not the same thing? It is the very nature of three and five and all the alternate integers that every one of them is invariably odd, although it is not identical with oddness. Similarly two and four and all the rest of the other series are not identical with even, but b each one of them always *is* even. Do you admit this, or not?

Of course I do.

Well, then, pay careful attention to the point which I want to make, which is this. It seems clear that the opposites themselves do not admit one another, but it also looks as though any things which, though not themselves opposites, always have opposites in them, similarly do not admit the opposite form to that which is in them, but on its approach either cease to exist or retire before it. Surely we must assert that three will sooner cease to exist or suffer any c other fate than submit to become even while it is still three?

Certainly, said Cebes.

And yet two and three are not opposites.

No, they are not.

So it is not only the opposite forms that cannot face one another's approach; there are other things too which cannot face the approach of opposites.

That is quite true.

Shall we try, if we can, to define what sort of things these are?
By all means.

d   Well, then, Cebes, would this describe them—that they are things which are compelled by some form which takes possession of them to assume not only its own form but invariably also that of some other form which is an opposite?
What do you mean?
Just what we were saying a minute ago. You realize, I suppose, that when the form of three takes possession of any group of objects, it compels them to be odd as well as three.
Certainly.
Then I maintain that into such a group the opposite form to the one which has this effect can never enter.
No, it cannot.
And it was the form of odd that had this effect?
Yes.
And the opposite of this is the form of even?
Yes.

e   So the form of even will never enter into three.
No, never.
In other words, three is incompatible with evenness.
Quite.
So the number three is uneven.
Yes.
I proposed just now to define what sort of things they are which, although they are not themselves directly opposed to a given opposite, nevertheless do not admit it, as in the present example, three, although not the opposite of even, nevertheless does not admit it, because three is always accompanied by the opposite of even—and similarly with two and odd, or fire and cold, and hosts of others. Well, see
105 whether you accept this definition. Not only does an opposite not admit its opposite, but if anything is accompanied by a form which has an opposite, and meets that opposite, then the thing which is accompanied never admits the opposite of the form by which it is accompanied. Let me refresh your memory; there is no harm in hearing a thing several times. Five will not admit the form of even, nor will ten, which is double five, admit the form of odd. Double has an opposite of its own, but at the same time it will not admit the form of
b   odd. Nor will one and a half, or other fractions such as one half or three quarters and so on, admit the form of whole. I assume that you follow me and agree.
I follow and agree perfectly, said Cebes.
Then run over the same ground with me from the beginning, and don't answer in the exact terms of the question, but follow my example. I say this because besides the 'safe answer' that I described at first, as the result of this discussion I now see another means of safety.

Suppose, for instance, that you ask me what must be present in body to make it hot. I shall not return the safe but ingenuous answer that it c is heat, but a more sophisticated one, based on the results of our discussion—namely that it is fire. And if you ask what must be present in a body to make it diseased, I shall say not disease but fever. Similarly if you ask what must be present in a number to make it odd, I shall say not oddness but unity, and so on. See whether you have a sufficient grasp now of what I want from you.

Quite sufficient.

Then tell me, what must be present in a body to make it alive?

Soul.

Is this always so?   d

Of course.

So whenever soul takes possession of a body, it always brings life with it?

Yes, it does.

Is there an opposite to life, or not?

Yes, there is.

What?

Death.

Does it follow, then, from our earlier agreement, that soul will never admit the opposite of that which accompanies it?

Most definitely, said Cebes.

Well, now, what name did we apply just now to that which does not admit the form of even?

Uneven.

And what do we call that which does not admit justice, or culture?

Uncultured, and the other unjust.   e

Very good. And what do we call that which does not admit death?

Immortal.

And soul does not admit death?

No.

So soul is immortal.

Yes, it is immortal.

Well, said Socrates, can we say that that has been proved? What do you think?

Most completely, Socrates.

Here is another question for you, Cebes. If the uneven were necessarily imperishable, would not three be imperishable?   106

Of course.

Then again, if what is not hot were necessarily imperishable, when you applied heat to snow, would not the snow withdraw still intact and unmelted? It could not cease to exist, nor on the other hand could it remain where it was and admit the heat.

That is true.

In the same way I assume that if what is not cold were imperishable, when anything cold approached fire, it could never go out or cease to exist; it would depart and be gone unharmed.

That must be so.

b   Are we not bound to say the same of the immortal? If what is immortal is also imperishable, it is impossible that at the approach of death soul should cease to be. It follows from what we have already said that it cannot admit death, or be dead—just as we said that three cannot be even, nor can odd; nor can fire be cold, nor can the heat which is in the fire. But, it may be objected, granting, as has been agreed, that odd does not become even at the approach of even, why should it not cease to exist, and something even take its place? In

c reply to this we could not insist that the odd does not cease to exist—because what is not even is not imperishable—but if this were conceded, we could easily insist that, at the approach of even, odd and three retire and depart. And we could be equally insistent about fire and heat and all the rest of them, could we not?

Certainly.

So now in the case of the immortal, if it is conceded that this is also imperishable, soul will be imperishable as well as immortal.

d Otherwise we shall need another argument.

There is no need on that account, said Cebes. If what is immortal and eternal cannot avoid destruction, it is hard to see how anything else can.

And I imagine that it would be admitted by everyone, said Socrates, that God at any rate, and the form of life, and anything else that is immortal, can never cease to exist.

Yes indeed, by all men certainly, and even more, I suppose, by the gods.

e   Then since what is immortal is also indestructible, if soul is really immortal, surely it must be imperishable too.

Quite inevitably.

So it appears that when death comes to a man, the mortal part of him dies, but the immortal part retires at the approach of death and escapes unharmed and indestructible.

Evidently.

Then it is as certain as anything can be, Cebes, that soul is im-

107 mortal and imperishable, and that our souls will really exist in the next world.

Well, Socrates, said Cebes, for my part I have no criticisms, and no doubt about the truth of your argument. But if Simmias here or anyone else has any criticism to make, he had better not keep it to himself, because if anyone wants to say or hear any more about this subject, I don't see to what other occasion he is to defer it.

As a matter of fact, said Simmias, I have no doubts myself either now, in view of what you have just been saying. All the same, the

subject is so vast, and I have such a poor opinion of our weak human b
nature, that I can't help still feeling some misgivings.

Quite right, Simmias, said Socrates, and what is more, even if
you find our original assumptions convincing, they still need more accurate consideration. If you and your friends examine them closely
enough, I believe that you will arrive at the truth of the matter, in so
far as it is possible for the human mind to attain it, and if you are sure
that you have done this, you will not need to inquire further.

That is true, said Simmias.

But there is a further point, gentlemen, said Socrates, which de- c
serves your attention. If the soul is immortal, it demands our care not
only for that part of time which we call life, but for all time. And indeed it would seem now that it will be extremely dangerous to neglect
it. If death were a release from everything, it would be a boon for the
wicked, because by dying they would be released not only from the
body but also from their own wickedness together with the soul, but
as it is, since the soul is clearly immortal, it can have no escape or security from evil except by becoming as good and wise as it possibly d
can. For it takes nothing with it to the next world except its education
and training, and these, we are told, are of supreme importance in
helping or harming the newly dead at the very beginning of his journey there.

This is how the story goes. When any man dies, his own guardian
spirit, which was given charge over him in his life, tries to bring him
to a certain place where all must assemble, and from which, after submitting their several cases to judgment, they must set out for the
next world, under the guidance of one who has the office of escorting e
souls from this world to the other. When they have there undergone
the necessary experiences and remained as long as is required, another guide brings them back again after many vast periods of time.

Of course this journey is not as Aeschylus makes Telephus describe it. He says that the path to Hades is straightforward, but it 108
seems clear to me that it is neither straightforward nor single. If it
were, there would be no need for a guide, because surely nobody could
lose his way anywhere if there were only one road. In fact, it seems
likely that it contains many forkings and crossroads, to judge from
the ceremonies and observances of this world.

Well, the wise and disciplined soul follows its guide and is not ignorant of its surroundings, but the soul which is deeply attached to
the body, as I said before, hovers round it and the visible world for a b
long time, and it is only after much resistance and suffering that it is
at last forcibly led away by its appointed guardian spirit. And when
it reaches the same place as the rest, the soul which is impure through
having done some impure deed, either by setting its hand to lawless
bloodshed or by committing other kindred crimes which are the work
of kindred souls, this soul is shunned and avoided by all. None will

c company with it or guide it, and it wanders alone in utter desolation until certain times have passed, whereupon it is borne away of necessity to its proper habitation. But every soul that has lived throughout its life in purity and soberness enjoys divine company and guidance, and each inhabits the place which is proper to it. There are many wonderful regions in the earth, and the earth itself is neither in nature nor in size such as geographers suppose it to be—so someone has assured me.

d   How can you say that, Socrates? said Simmias. I myself have heard a great many theories about the earth, but not this belief of yours. I should very much like to hear it.

Why, really, Simmias, I don't think that it calls for the skill of a Glaucus to explain what my belief is, but to prove that it is true seems to me to be too difficult even for a Glaucus. In the first place I should probably be unable to do it, and in the second, even if I knew how, it seems to me, Simmias, that my life is too short for a long explanation. However, there is no reason why I should not tell you what I believe
e about the appearance of the earth and regions in it.

Well, said Simmias, even that will do.

This is what I believe, then, said Socrates. In the first place, if the earth is spherical and in the middle of the heavens, it needs neither
109 air nor any other such force to keep it from falling; the uniformity of the heavens and the equilibrium of the earth itself are sufficient to support it. Any body in equilibrium, if it is set in the middle of a uniform medium, will have no tendency to sink or rise in any direction more than another, and having equal impulses will remain suspended. This is the first article of my belief.

And quite right too, said Simmias.

Next, said Socrates, I believe that it is vast in size, and that we
b who dwell between the river Phasis and the Pillars of Hercules inhabit only a minute portion of it—we live round the sea like ants or frogs round a pond—and there are many other peoples inhabiting similar regions. There are many hollow places all round the earth, places of every shape and size, into which the water and mist and air have collected. But the earth itself is as pure as the starry heaven in which it
c lies, and which is called aether by most of our authorities. The water, mist, and air are the dregs of this aether, and they are continually draining into the hollow places in the earth. We do not realize that we are living in its hollows, but assume that we are living on the earth's surface. Imagine someone living in the depths of the sea. He might think that he was living on the surface, and seeing the sun and the other heavenly bodies through the water; he might think that the sea was the sky. He might be so sluggish and feeble that he had never
d reached the top of the sea, never emerged and raised his head from the sea into this world of ours, and seen for himself—or even heard

from someone who had seen it—how much purer and more beautiful it really is than the one in which his people lives. Now we are in just the same position. Although we live in a hollow of the earth, we assume that we are living on the surface, and we call the air heaven, as though it were the heaven through which the stars move. And this point too is the same, that we are too feeble and sluggish to make our e way out to the upper limit of the air. If someone could reach to the summit, or put on wings and fly aloft, when he put up his head he would see the world above, just as fishes see our world when they put up their heads out of the sea. And if his nature were able to bear the sight, he would recognize that that is the true heaven and the true light and the true earth. For this earth and its stones and all the re- 110 gions in which we live are marred and corroded, just as in the sea everything is corroded by the brine, and there is no vegetation worth mentioning, and scarcely any degree of perfect formation, but only caverns and sand and measureless mud, and tracts of slime wherever there is earth as well, and nothing is in the least worthy to be judged beautiful by our standards. But the things above excel those of our world to a degree far greater still. If this is the right moment for an b imaginative description, Simmias, it will be worth your while to hear what it is really like upon the earth which lies beneath the heavens.

Yes, indeed, Socrates, said Simmias, it would be a great pleasure to us, at any rate, to hear this description.

Well, my dear boy, said Socrates, the real earth, viewed from above, is supposed to look like one of these balls made of twelve pieces of skin, variegated and marked out in different colors, of which the colors which we know are only limited samples, like the paints which artists use, but there the whole earth is made up of such colors, and c others far brighter and purer still. One section is a marvelously beautiful purple, and another is golden. All that is white of it is whiter than chalk or snow, and the rest is similarly made up of the other colors, still more and lovelier than those which we have seen. Even these very hollows in the earth, full of water and air, assume a kind of color as they gleam amid the different hues around them, so that there ap- d pears to be one continuous surface of varied colors. The trees and flowers and fruits which grow upon this earth are proportionately beautiful. The mountains too and the stones have a proportionate smoothness and transparency, and their colors are lovelier. The pebbles which are so highly prized in our world—the jaspers and rubies and emeralds and the rest—are fragments of these stones, but there e everything is as beautiful as they are, or better still. This is because the stones there are in their natural state, not damaged by decay and corroded by salt water as ours are by the sediment which has collected here, and which causes disfigurement and disease to stones and earth, and animals and plants as well. The earth itself is adorned not only

111 with all these stones but also with gold and silver and the other met-
als, for many rich veins of them occur in plain view in all parts of the
earth, so that to see them is a sight for the eyes of the blessed.

There are many kinds of animals upon it, and also human beings, some of whom live inland, others round the air, as we live round
the sea, and others in islands surrounded by air but close to the main-
land. In a word, as water and the sea are to us for our purposes, so is
b air to them, and as air is to us, so the æther is to them. Their climate is
so temperate that they are free from disease and live much longer
than people do here, and in sight and hearing and understanding and
all other faculties they are as far superior to us as air is to water or
æther to air in clarity.

They also have sanctuaries and temples which are truly inhab-
ited by gods, and oracles and prophecies and visions and all other
c kinds of communion with the gods occur there face to face. They see
the sun and moon and stars as they really are, and the rest of their
happiness is after the same manner.

Such is the nature of the earth as a whole and of the things that
are upon it. In the earth itself, all over its surface, there are many hollow regions, some deeper and more widely spread than that in which
we live, others deeper than our region but with a smaller expanse,
d some both shallower than ours and broader. All these are joined together underground by many connecting channels, some narrower,
some wider, through which, from one basin to another, there flows a
great volume of water—monstrous unceasing subterranean rivers of
waters both hot and cold—and of fire too, great rivers of fire, and many
of liquid mud, some clearer, some more turbid, like the rivers in Sicily
e that flow mud before the lava comes, and the lava stream itself. By
these the several regions are filled in turn as the flood reaches them.

All this movement to and fro is caused by an oscillation inside
the earth, and this oscillation is brought about by natural means, as
follows.

One of the cavities in the earth is not only larger than the rest,
but pierces right through from one side to the other. It is of this that
112 Homer speaks when he says, 'Far, far away, where lies earth's deep-
est chasm,' [2] while elsewhere both he and many other poets refer to it
as Tartarus. Into this gulf all the rivers flow together, and from it
they flow forth again, and each acquires the nature of that part of the
b earth through which it flows. The cause of the flowing in and out of
all these streams is that the mass of liquid has no bottom or foundation; so it oscillates and surges to and fro, and the air or breath that
belongs to it does the same, for it accompanies the liquid both as it
rushes to the further side of the earth and as it returns to this. And
just as when we breathe we exhale and inhale the breath in a continu-

[2] *Iliad* 8.14.

myself ridiculous in my own eyes if I clung to life and hugged it when it has no more to offer. Come, do as I say and don't make difficulties.

At this Crito made a sign to his servant, who was standing near by. The servant went out and after spending a considerable time returned with the man who was to administer the poison. He was carrying it ready-prepared in a cup.

When Socrates saw him he said, Well, my good fellow, you understand these things. What ought I to do?

Just drink it, he said, and then walk about until you feel a weight in your legs, and then lie down. Then it will act of its own accord. b

As he spoke he handed the cup to Socrates, who received it quite cheerfully, Echecrates, without a tremor, without any change of color or expression, and said, looking up under his brows with his usual steady gaze, What do you say about pouring a libation from this drink? Is it permitted, or not?

We only prepare what we regard as the normal dose, Socrates, he replied.

I see, said Socrates. But I suppose I am allowed, or rather bound, c to pray the gods that my removal from this world to the other may be prosperous. This is my prayer, then, and I hope that it may be granted.

With these words, quite calmly and with no sign of distaste, he drained the cup in one breath.

Up till this time most of us had been fairly successful in keeping back our tears, but when we saw that he was drinking, that he had actually drunk it, we could do so no longer. In spite of myself the tears came pouring out, so that I covered my face and wept brokenheartedly—not for him, but for my own calamity in losing such a friend. d Crito had given up even before me, and had gone out when he could not restrain his tears. But Apollodorus, who had never stopped crying even before, now broke out into such a storm of passionate weeping that he made everyone in the room break down, except Socrates himself, who said, Really, my friends, what a way to behave! Why, that was my main reason for sending away the women, to prevent this sort of disturbance, because I am told that one should make one's end in a e tranquil frame of mind. Calm yourselves and try to be brave.

This made us feel ashamed, and we controlled our tears. Socrates walked about, and presently, saying that his legs were heavy, lay down on his back—that was what the man recommended. The man — he was the same one who had administered the poison—kept his hand upon Socrates, and after a little while examined his feet and legs, then pinched his foot hard and asked if he felt it. Socrates said no. Then he did the same to his legs, and moving gradually upward in this 118 way let us see that he was getting cold and numb. Presently he felt him again and said that when it reached the heart, Socrates would be gone.

The coldness was spreading about as far as his waist when Socrates uncovered his face, for he had covered it up, and said—they were his last words—Crito, we ought to offer a cock to Asclepius. See to it, and don't forget.

No, it shall be done, said Crito. Are you sure that there is nothing else?

Socrates made no reply to this question, but after a little while he stirred, and when the man uncovered him, his eyes were fixed. When Crito saw this, he closed the mouth and eyes.

Such, Echecrates, was the end of our comrade, who was, we may fairly say, of all those whom we knew in our time, the bravest and also the wisest and most upright man.